# Cambridge Elements ≡

Elements in the Philosophy of Law
edited by
George Pavlakos
*University of Glasgow*
Gerald J. Postema
*University of North Carolina at Chapel Hill*
Kenneth M. Ehrenberg
*University of Surrey*

# THE PLACE OF COERCION
# IN LAW

Triantafyllos Gkouvas
*Universidad Carlos III de Madrid*

CAMBRIDGE
UNIVERSITY PRESS

Shaftesbury Road, Cambridge CB2 8EA, United Kingdom

One Liberty Plaza, 20th Floor, New York, NY 10006, USA

477 Williamstown Road, Port Melbourne, VIC 3207, Australia

314–321, 3rd Floor, Plot 3, Splendor Forum, Jasola District Centre, New Delhi – 110025, India

103 Penang Road, #05–06/07, Visioncrest Commercial, Singapore 238467

Cambridge University Press is part of Cambridge University Press & Assessment, a department of the University of Cambridge.

We share the University's mission to contribute to society through the pursuit of education, learning and research at the highest international levels of excellence.

www.cambridge.org
Information on this title: www.cambridge.org/9781009009638

DOI: 10.1017/9781009008167

First published 2023

*A catalogue record for this publication is available from the British Library.*

ISBN 978-1-009-00963-8 Paperback
ISSN 2631-5815 (online)
ISSN 2631-5807 (print)

# The Place of Coercion in Law

Elements in the Philosophy of Law

DOI: 10.1017/9781009008167
First published online: March 2023

Triantafyllos Gkouvas
*Universidad Carlos III de Madrid*

**Author for correspondence:** Triantafyllos Gkouvás, tr.gouvas@gmail.com

**Abstract:** The question of whether coercion is a necessary or contingent feature of governance by law is a historically complex aspect of a venerable 'modalist' trend in jurisprudential thinking. The nature of the relation between law and coercion has been elaborated by means of a variety of modally qualified accounts, all converging in a more or less committing response to whether the language, concept or essence of law as a system of governance necessarily entails the coercive character of this system. This Element remodels in non-modal terms the way in which legal philosophers can meaningfully disagree about the coercive character of governance by law. On this alternative model, there can be no meaningful disagreement about whether law is coercive without prior agreement on the contours of a theory of how law is made.

**Keywords:** coercion, normativity, modality, disagreement, lawmaking

ISBNs: 9781009009638 (PB), 9781009008167 (OC)
ISSNs: 2631-5815 (online), 2631-5807 (print)

# Contents

## Introduction

The familiarity of analytic jurisprudence with articulating metaphysical questions in modal terms is old enough to merit a legacy of its own. Familiar scenarios include cases where the enforcement of law is undertaken by a morally wicked regime or, conversely, cases where an angelic society is governed by laws which are not backed by legal sanctions. Traditionally, investigations of modality concentrate on propositions about which things could or could not have been true in a variety of ways – metaphysical, epistemic, nomic, biological, normative. In the spirit of evaluating the truth of propositions by reference to how 'secure' it remains in scenarios that are alternative to the way things actually are, legal philosophers have been keen on testing the tenacity of jurisprudential truths across a broad spectrum of alternative ways in which governance by law can be manifested. Accordingly, the record of modal questions in analytical jurisprudence is richer in scope than what is suggested by a single abstract question about the relation between law and morality.

The question of whether coercion is a necessary or contingent feature of governance by law is a historically complex aspect of this 'modalist' trend in jurisprudential thinking. This trend is not just about settling the question of whether law is necessarily or contingently coercive, or whether law is necessarily or contingently morally justified. It is also about the question of whether the law necessarily or contingently emerges from the actions and practices of the state, whether law necessarily or contingently has a distributional role in matters of justice, as well as whether legal authority is necessarily or contingently compatible with individual freedom.[1]

The nature of the relation between law and coercion has been elaborated by means of a variety of modally qualified accounts, all converging in a more or less committing response to whether the language, concept or essence of law as a system of governance *necessarily* entails the coercive character of this system. The necessity of a legal system's coercive character is mainly the concern of social, legal and political theorists and philosophers of law. But necessity in itself can only be conceptualised, described or otherwise contemplated. It cannot be measured, observed, anticipated or used in the way we use tangible objects as tools. In a layperson's life, it matters little whether a legal system's ability to inhibit certain behaviours or the exercise of this ability in real space and time are necessitated by the nature of law as a system of governance.

---

[1] If asked about what most poignantly marks this modalist strategy, an analytically trained legal philosopher would most likely respond by singling out H.L.A. Hart's avidly debated *separation thesis* as a peak manifestation of this philosophical trend. *See* H.L.A. HART, THE CONCEPT OF LAW (2d ed. 1994).

Accordingly – and this is what our mundane observations or predictions about the actions of legal institutions enable us to infer – a particular legal system's coercive character will combine, to varying degrees, elements of possible and actual coercion depending on the political history of its emergence, on the economic prosperity and political stability of its society, as well as on the smoothness of its interaction with other local systems of normative guidance (religion, social morality, culture, etiquette etc.). Sometimes a legal system's coercive character will rely to a greater extent on how the possibility of its use of coercive means induces the conformity of its subjects to norms backed up by sanctions. In some other times and contexts, the actual punishment of lawbreakers and the direct use of physical force may become the main avenue for inducing compliance.

The Element will focus on the non-observational or theoretical aspect of coercion in governance by law, and compare the ways in which foundational theories of law accommodate within their premises ideas about the importance and nature of coercion in governance by law. It will focus on governance by law in its manifestation in the operations of legal systems rather than on the typology of the norms that legal systems produce. In other words, we will not be exploring the question of whether individual legal norms necessitate an explicit or implicit coercive complement (threat of sanction) in their logical regimentation.

In focusing on systems of governance by law, the Element will not draw its guiding assumptions from the phenomenology of how actual persons synchronically experience and how actual societies diachronically internalise the idea that law is coercive. It will also not draw its inspiration from idealisations or rationalisations of this phenomenology as often happens when we think of the exemplary, socio-politically representative, ideally rational or pedestrianly morally bad person who lives in a law-governed society. Both approaches are powerfully revealing and instructive in their own ways, but they fall short of registering the metaphysical dimension across which foundational theories of law argue about the necessity of recognising enforceable constraints in the nature and operation of legal systems. Accordingly, this will be a text on legal metaphysics.

There is no accident in how the modal-metaphysical trend of necessary and contingent features developed its own research agenda – for the simple reason that the logic of necessity and possibility is flexible enough to be used for testing the counterfactual tenacity of different types of argument including, most prominently, semantic, conceptual, essentialist and probabilistic claims about the coercive nature of legal systems. Despite its venerable pedigree in classical theories of law such as John Austin's imperatival theory of legal obligation and

Hans Kelsen's pure theory of law, the modal-metaphysical articulation of the question of whether governance by law is coercive is already a very advanced step in the more general discussion about the nature of law.

It would be more instructive to see this modal-metaphysical framework as the (still trending) *outcome* of a long history of commendable methodological efforts to enrich scholarly research in general jurisprudence rather than as the easiest or most forthcoming way to begin an instructive entry on the coercive character of law. The purpose of this entry-like Element is not to dispute the instructional value of this outcome nor to dispute its conceptual origins but to complement the context in which theories of law part ways when they reach the end point of making a modal statement about whether law is necessarily coercive.

To obtain a more global command of the issue of whether coercion is a necessary or contingent feature of law we need to equip our inquiry with a metaphysically inclusive vocabulary that will enable a jurisprudentially unseasoned or non-committed reader to infer and, most importantly, *compare* the ontological commitments of modally articulated views on the jurisprudential importance of coercion. Such comparison may not always be instantly available precisely because, as I will try to show, the metaphysical commitments of competing modal accounts of law's coerciveness are often irreconcilable, orthogonal or somehow incommensurable.

The aim of this Element is to propose and defend a reconfiguration of the terms in which legal philosophers can genuinely and productively disagree about the coercive character of governance by law. In the course of approaching this aim, I will not be advocating an alternative or hybrid theory of the jurisprudential importance of coercion. Instead, I will proceed in two steps, only the second of which marks a real departure from available ways of framing this dispute.

The first step will be to regroup in a taxonomically simple way a cohort of prominent theories on the jurisprudential importance of coercion, based on whether they treat coercion as an aspect of the axiological or deontic dimension of law. In Section 1, I will treat these two aspects (axiological and deontic) as the two halves of an axis I will be referring to as the 'perspectival axis'. Both halves operate as a practical perspective from which different verdicts on the modal profile of coercion can be reached. The axiological half will be taken to portray governance by law as a uniquely equipped instrument for promoting certain social, moral and political values. The deontic half will be taken to portray law as an answer to the question of what rights and duties we have as members of a political society. I will treat this taxonomic axis as the shortest avenue for introducing newcomers to the debate on the coercive nature of legal systems.

In Section 2, taking a more controversial step, I will replace the modal question of whether governance by law is necessarily or contingently coercive with what I will describe as the *metric* question of the extent to which propositions about the legal relevance of situations of state coercion are inexorably true. Inexorability will be understood as resistance to falsification and legal relevance will be understood as a way of being legally normative.[2] Truths that admit of degrees of inexorability, I will argue, are essentially relative to what a given theory treats as the legally relevant actuality. In the legal case this actuality will be equated with the reality of how law is made. Relative to the relevant actuality, some truths will be more inexorable the more difficult it is for them to be falsified when the context in which they still hold gradually becomes more different from the actual context. Accordingly, the metric question turns the determination of the jurisprudential importance of coercion into a comparative issue. The degree of difficulty for a truth about the legal relevance of state coercion to fail to be true will depend on the range of situations that are alternative to what a given theory treats as the actuality of how law is made where this proposition *remains* true.

In Section 3 I will combine this new question with an updated taxonomic model that is two- instead of one-dimensional. Besides the dimension composed of the deontic and axiological perspective, I will add a second ontological dimension on which a theory can be located with respect to whether it chooses to individuate legal practices on descriptive or, conversely, normative grounds. With this new question, and thanks to the addition of a second taxonomic dimension, I will try to make visible the extent to which legal philosophers who are keen on debating the coercive character of law are likely to be talking past each other.

The metric question about the jurisprudential importance of coercion can assist us in distinguishing meaningful from verbal episodes of disagreement because any eligible answer to this type of question is sensitive to how each theory draws the boundary that separates *this* theory's 'law' from *this* theory's *schlaw*. *Schlegal* disagreements are not meaningful disagreements and there will be occasions when *theory A*'s 'legal' – jurisprudentially important – coercion is *theory B*'s *schegal* coercion. All jurisprudential theories draw such inner boundaries in more or less explicit ways and these boundaries are the last to be crossed or redrawn when progress is made in some deep disagreement.

---

[2] Legal normativity need not be seen as an irreducible normative phenomenon. There exist jurisprudential theories that analyse legal normativity in rational, moral, prudential or political terms. Most importantly, legal normativity need not and will not be confined to the normativity of providing justifying (moral) or motivating (prudential) reasons for action.

Most importantly, crossing these boundaries without prior consensus between jurisprudential interlocutors may transform the dispute into a parallel monologue, or so I would like to argue. Many would make haste to dismiss as idiosyncratic or unfounded my suspicion about the meaningfulness of jurisprudential disagreement. There are plentiful occasions where legal philosophers have been productively engaging in long disputes about the coercive character of law. Their exchanges cannot be Babelian. My concern, however, is not motivated by observations of systematic miscommunication of such biblical proportions. The spectre of parallel monologues does not loom as widely over our community as my initial comment may have erroneously suggested. There is a good reason for this auspicious estimation and this reason, I believe, remains suppressed. It relates to how the boundary between 'law' and 'schlaw' is handled by jurisprudential interlocutors.

Disagreements between jurisprudential experts on the role of coercion in law can be productive, and are often relatively easy to resolve, mitigate or adjudicate when and because parties to a dispute are careful not to trespass the boundary that separates *this* theory's 'law' from *this* theory's *schlaw*. Such boundaries can be, and often are, common. They need not be set by each theory separately and they need not demarcate the conceptual region of one theory at a time. The criteria for drawing these boundaries can be articulated at such a high level of abstraction that they become *inter*-jurisprudential: they can be recombined and specified to such an extent and in a such a way that allows different theories to draw the *same* boundaries while remaining jurisprudentially irreconcilable on familiar issues including the role of morality in law and the political dimension of law.

Accordingly, the sceptical ambience conveyed by my words is misleading and any suspicion of pervasive miscommunication about the jurisprudential importance of coercion is indeed misplaced. What is not misplaced is the much narrower concern that, for lack of a common inter-jurisprudential boundary, advocates of *certain* theories cannot directly engage in meaningful disputes about the coerciveness of law without consenting to a prior reconstruction of their views on what makes governance by law typical. In Section 2 I will associate this typicality with a theory's conception of how law is made. A theory of lawmaking, I will argue, is a conceptual precursor to a jurisprudential theory of coercion.

That being said, I remain humbly aware of the fact that many readers will not be eager to endorse my intuitions as evidentially basic for our understanding of how legal philosophers disagree about the coercive character of law. For instance, they may think that I inject unnecessary preconditions into what could otherwise operate as a useful guide to theoretical disagreement over the jurisprudential importance of state coercion. Why, in this regard, should questions about how law is made figure essentially in the explanation of whether coercion is jurisprudentially important? Other readers may feel inclined to set off the 'Ockhamite' alarm by suggesting that, other things being equal, I should be looking for a much simpler explanation of why certain disagreements about the jurisprudential importance of coercion tend to become inscrutable or unamenable to principled adjudication. In this regard, a valid worry is that by introducing the concept of legal relevance as a qualifier of both facts about state coercion and facts about how law is made, I have turned a discussion about the jurisprudential importance of coercion into a much broader discussion about legal normativity.

In default of an early or easy response to such valid concerns I can only invite readers to consider accepting the application of my proposed taxonomy to the original modal question of whether coercion is a necessary or contingent feature of governance by law. Crucially, this way of using the model can operate independently of its repurposing for addressing the metric question. Any decision to embrace or provisionally consider my metric approach as a step forward will depend on how well I fare in foregrounding the virtues of my approach. Does the metric approach offer a better explanation of existing problems than the modal approach or does it fabricate a new problem that has the semblance of an existing problem? This remains to be seen.

## 1 A Taxonomy for a Modal Question

My proposal for constructing a taxonomy of jurisprudential views on the necessity or contingency of law's coerciveness is based on the idea that the question of whether governance by law is necessarily or contingently coercive is *perspectival* in a practical sense. This is to say that the truth of judgements about the necessity or contingency of coercion as an aspect of the nature and operation of legal systems depends on which practical standpoint is occupied by someone who judges coercion to be a necessary or contingent feature of governance by law. For the purposes of this question, I will single out two very broad types of practical perspective: a *deontic* perspective and an *axiological* perspective.

In general, the phrase 'practical standpoint' purports to capture those features of an individual or collective agent's practical judgements, values and the like on which the truth of *further, derivative* judgements depends. These can be modal judgements about what is necessarily or contingently true of a social, moral, legal or political practice or normative judgements about what one ought or has reason to do, think or feel or which state of affairs is worthy of promotion. The relevant relation between a practical perspective and perspectival propositions is that of *logical entailment*. This is a non-normative, at least in any robust sense, relation holding between the propositions expressed by the respective judgements.[3]

Accordingly, propositions about the necessity or contingency of law's coerciveness will be reinterpreted as *derivative propositions* that are logically entailed from a certain practical perspective. Such derivative propositions can have a conceptual, metaphysical, normative, semantic, doxastic or other type of flavour depending on the type of necessity or contingency that a given theory takes on board. The practical perspective from which claims of conceptual, metaphysical, normative, semantic or doxastic necessity or contingency follow can be respectively endowed with conceptual, metaphysical, normative, semantic or doxastic elements. Both the deontic and axiological variants of a practical perspective on the modal profile of coercion are pliable enough to be further specified by different theories as involving assumptions about deontic or axiological *concepts*, deontic or axiological *properties*, deontic or axiological *norms*, deontic or axiological *language*, deontic or axiological *beliefs* and so on.

Before infusing this type of perspective with some content it is important to note that occupying a practical–normative perspective does not commit a legal theorist to a non-positivist account of the nature of law. Locutions like 'A has a legal obligation to $\phi$', 'A legally ought to $\phi$', '*not $\phi$-ing* is illegal' or 'the law requires that one $\phi$ in circumstances C' are used interchangeably in the context of our reports of what the content of the law is or entails in a given circumstance. As one may reasonably expect, it is legal positivists who bear the brunt of accommodating the use of normative or prescriptive language in law in a way that does not vitiate their core commitment to how descriptive facts make law. In the service of disassociating what the law is from what the law ought to be,

---

[3]   Sharon Street outlines the role of entailment in perspectival normative judgements noting that

> [q]uite apart from whether we think a given set of values is correct, in other words – indeed, even if we aren't clear yet on what it is for a set of values to be *correct* – we can nevertheless think about and discuss what *follows*, as a purely logical and instrumental matter, from a given set of values in combination with the non-normative facts. Sharon Street, *Constructivism in Ethics and Metaethics*, 5 Philos. Compass 363, 367 (2010).

It is a further metasemantic question whether the perspective-dependence of normative judgements is a consequence of the manner in which the *content* or, conversely, the *truth-conditions* of a normative judgement are determined by the relevant perspective. In the former case, normative judgements are treated as indexically anchored to a given perspective, whereas in the latter case the same type of judgement is treated as metasemantically perspectival. For this distinction, see Karl Schafer, *Constructivism and Three Forms of Perspective-Dependence in Metaethics*, 89 Philos. Phenomenol. Res. 69, 69–71 (2012) and John MacFarlane, *Nonindexical Contextualism*, 166 Synthese 231 (2009).

analytic legal positivism offers an impressive gamut of linguistic frameworks for accommodating the normative flavour of legal discourse.[4]

The first jurisprudential perspective that I will single out for the purposes of our taxonomic quest is the *deontic* perspective of an agent who treats a system of governance by law as a distinct source of duties and rights. This perspective assesses the truth of modal propositions about the jurisprudential necessity or contingency of coercion as an aspect of the *deontic function* of governance by law. This is to say, it represents the coercive practices of law as *deontically* necessary or *deontically* contingent aspects of governance by law. Coercion can be a deontically necessary aspect of law in different ways. For instance, it may be a necessary aspect of institutional responses to legal wrongdoing or a necessary aspect of legal authority.[5] The same applies to ways for coercion to be a deontically contingent aspect of law. The actual use of collective force by the state can impose limits on the legitimacy of legal authority but these limits could easily be absent if other non-coercive means of compliance were prioritised.[6] The deontic perspective is not exclusively applicable to explanations of why law is necessarily or contingently coercive. It figures essentially in any jurisprudential explanation of why we ought to obey the law, or why treating each other in certain ways is legally impermissible, or why we bear certain legal obligations and entitlements and not others.

The second jurisprudential perspective is the *axiological* perspective of an agent who treats a system of governance by law as a valuable instrument for promoting certain basic values that exist independently of the system's normative force and help to shape the public political culture of a society.[7] It figures

---

[4] For two distinct positivist accounts of the legal point of view, see Triantafyllos Gkouvas, *Resisting Perspectivalism about Law: The Scope of Jurisprudential Disagreement*, 8 Jurisprudence 205, 211–17 (2017).

[5] Kantian theories of law are typical examples of this approach. See, for instance, Ernest Weinrib, Corrective Justice (2012); Arthur Ripstein, *As if It Had Never Happened*, 48 Wm. & Mary L. Rev. 1957 (2007); Christopher Essert, *From Raz's Nexus to Legal Normativity*, 25 Can. J. L. & Jurisprudence 465 (2012).

[6] Lucas Miotto advances a contingentist view by relying on a distinctly deontic perspective: the perspective of *reasonableness*. In his words,

> most philosophers accept that enforcement mechanisms are coercive only if they make non-compliance with legal mandates unreasonable in some non-trivial sense (to be specified by an account of coercion). That coerciveness is not tantamount to the presence of sanctions and enforcement mechanisms and *that a legal system is coercive only when the enforcement mechanisms render non-compliance with legal mandates unreasonable in some non-trivial sense is all an argument for the contingency of coerciveness in legal systems needs* [emphasis added]. Lucas Miotto, *From Angels to Humans: Law, Coercion, and the Society of Angels Thought Experiment*, 40 Law and Philosophy 277, 296 (2021).

[7] 'Axiological' is often treated as synonymous with *value-theoretical*. Francesco Orsi gives a pithy description of the axiological dimension of value inquiry. In his words, it

essentially in any jurisprudential explanation of why certain actions of legal institutions best promote the values which a given theory of law treats as ideally served by legal-institutional means. This is to say, it represents the coercive practices of law as *axiologically* necessary or *axiologically* contingent aspects of governance by law. Coercion can be an axiologically necessary aspect of law in different ways. For instance, coercion can be a necessary aspect of the way a legal system prevents the bad consequences of relapsing into a state of nature.[8] The same applies to ways in which coercion can be an axiologically contingent aspect of law. Governance by law can be theorised as being contrived in such a way that it promotes a plurality of values but whether, when and for how long it so promotes them remains an empirical issue.[9]

## 1.1 The Axiological Perspective

Given the historical depth of instrumental conceptions of law's relation to moral and political values it is inevitable that significant fluctuations in the standards by which law's instrumental value is 'measured' will be witnessed, as well as in the language in which such coercively realised values are described. Moreover, the gamut of available specifications of the values which state coercion is tasked with promoting is also a powerful indication that legal theory's evolutionary trajectory is constantly tracking the parallel evolution of ideas regarding the relationship between law and the state. It is only against this volatile background that reasons of taxonomic neutrality make strongly advisable the avoidance of general remarks about the existence of an underlying pattern in the development of ideas about law's axiology.

---

stands for all substantive views about what is fundamentally good and bad, and the debate among them. For instance, hedonism is a value theory, holding that pleasure is the one fundamental positive value. As such, it is opposed to other theories, e.g. perfectionism, holding that the excellent development of certain abilities is the fundamental positive value, or to some pluralist theory, holding that there is more than one fundamental value, for example pleasure, knowledge, and moral virtue. FRANCESCO ORSI, VALUE THEORY 6 (2015).

[8] Hobbesian theories of law are typical examples of this approach. For recent contributions to this approach, see Andrew Stumpff Morrison, *Law Is the Command of the Sovereign: H.L.A. Hart Reconsidered*, 29 RATIO JURIS. 364 (2016). For a non-Hobbesian, conceptual-axiological approach, see KENNETH EINAR HIMMA, COERCION AND THE NATURE OF LAW (2020). In Section 1.1, I go into greater detail about Himma's axiological necessitarian approach and the importance he assigns to the value of social and political peace. Crucially, the value or values advocated in support of law's necessary coercive function need not be substantial. They can also be formal or institutional. Values like the settlement of disputes or consistency in action can play this role. For the latter view, see Joseph D'Agostino, *Law's Necessary Violence*, 22 TEX. REV. LAW POLITICS 121, 172 (2017).

[9] *See* FREDERICK SCHAUER, THE FORCE OF LAW (2015). Also, in Section 1.1, I provide a short analysis of Schauer's axiological contingentist approach.

All available specifications of the axiological perspective treat law as a means for promoting states of affairs that are, or are taken to be, independently valuable and hence worthy of legal protection or promotion. Perhaps to the dismay of twentieth-century legal positivists, the forefathers of early legal positivism like Jeremy Bentham and John Austin were not coy about treating as supremely valuable states of affairs as prosaic or blunt as the interests and longevous reign of the sovereign. It goes without saying that without backing as many legal norms as possible with the threat of sanctions imposed by the political sovereign the project of upholding the sovereignty of a state would have dim prospects. The threat of sanctions is prudentially recommendable for securing the habitual obedience of legal imperatives and such habitual obedience is a necessary means for protecting the interests of sovereignty.[10]

It bears noting that the axiological theorisation of law goes beyond its empirical efficacy in bringing about certain outcomes including the enforcement of habitual obedience. Standard appeals to the general efficacy of law encode a general assumption about the existence conditions of legal systems. Most if not all legal philosophers agree that legal systems exist only if their laws are normally obeyed. Efficacy construed as general obedience can be attained by a varying mixture of official coercion, habit, acceptance of the moral legitimacy of the law and social peer pressure. By contrast, 'efficacy' construed as promotion of certain independently valuable states of affairs does not concern the empirically confirmed capacity of legal institutions to secure general obedience through coercive or other means; rather, it concerns their capacity as a matter of their conceptual or normative design to realise either a list of more basic values or an overarching value such as security, stability or peace in relation to which general obedience is only an empirical condition.

Frederick Schauer advances a *contingentist* version of the 'list-approach'. In his recent monograph, *The Force of Law*, he leaves no doubt about the orientation of his jurisprudential take on coercion. For Schauer, law is 'commonly and

---

[10] *See* JEREMY BENTHAM, A FRAGMENT OF GOVERNMENT 109 (1988). John Austin's imperatival theory of law provides a typical defence of the jurisprudential importance of sanctions as prudential reasons for obedience. *See* JOHN AUSTIN, THE PROVINCE OF JURISPRUDENCE DETERMINED (Wilfrid E. Rumble ed., 1832, 1995). For a neo-Austinian account of the role of sanctions and the use of force in law, see Frederick Schauer, *Was Austin Right After All? On the Role of Sanctions in a Theory of Law*, 23 RATIO JURIS. 1 (2010). Ekow Yankah draws a distinction between sanctioning and coercing behaviour and claims that if something is necessarily coercive about law as a system of action-guiding norms it is the use of physical force by the law, not as an end in itself but as a means to compel individuals to take or refrain from taking some action. In his words, '[t]he ability to use coercion under special conditions defines legal norms. Legal philosophy is, to borrow a phrase, philosophy with bayonets.' Ekow Yankah, *The Force of Law: The Role of Coercion in Legal Norms*, 42 U. RICH. L. REV. 1195, 1197 (2008).

*valuably* [emphasis added] coercive'.[11] Schauer's axiological perspective is informed by empirical observations about how governance by law is actually mobilised. Law is often used to motivate people to endorse in their judgements and actions a collective sense of good policy or wise choice and more often than not this process will be enabled by forcing them to do so. Schauer is not an essentialist or conceptualist about the attributes of a legal system, hence he prefers to remain non-committal with respect to the range of values served by typical legal systems. This is evident when he notes that

> coercion is neither necessary nor sufficient for law. But legal coercion's contingent ubiquity testifies to the fact that in many domains there are *valuable goals* that cannot be achieved by cooperation alone, even the kind of cooperation in which people internalize second-order reasons for suppressing their first-order desires and decisions. If we ignore this fact, we will have ignored something very important about why law exists and what functions it serves [emphasis added].[12]

By sharp contrast, Kenneth Himma provides a conceptually *necessitarian* defence of the latter approach. Himma sees the practices constitutive of a legal system as uniquely and rationally contrived to 'minimize breaches of the peace only insofar as they back legal norms prohibiting such breaches with the threat of a coercive sanction'.[13] Peace is the overarching value that fuels with content an axiological perspective from which governance by law is represented as conceptually necessary. According to Himma's *coercion thesis*, 'it is a conceptually necessary condition for something to count as a system of law that it is reasonably contrived to keep the *peace* [emphasis added]' and 'it is a conceptual truth that every legal system authorizes coercive sanctions for *some* non-official acts that breach the *peace*' [emphasis added].[14]

Because Himma takes it to be a conceptual truth that governance by law is geared towards preventing breaches of social peace, it follows that it is also conceptually true that the peace-centred axiological perspective is the only apt perspective from which to assess the jurisprudential importance of the legally authorised means for keeping peace. In his words, '[a]n institutional normative system is not reasonably contrived to regulate behavior unless the peace is kept enough for subjects to live together in a community'.[15]

Another contemporary account of the contingent role that coercion plays in a legal system is the facilitation of peoples' response to antecedent morally good reasons. Instead of using coercion to necessitate people's response to the commands of the sovereign, the coercive operations of certain legal institutions

---

[11] SCHAUER, *supra* note 9, at x.   [12] *Id.* at 165.   [13] HIMMA, *supra* note 8, at 19.
[14] *Id.* at 73 and 15, respectively.   [15] *Id.* at 16.

can simply facilitate people's responsiveness to reasons that apply to them independently of the say-so of the sovereign. Such facilitation is a contingent matter because not every conceivable scenario needs such facilitation to rest on coercive means. For this reason, such an approach does not assign to coercion the status of a necessary feature of law. A good example of this approach is Joseph Raz who portrays the coercive aspect of the actions of law-applying institutions as a sufficient but not necessary way of seeing to it that law subjects are induced to respond to good reasons that apply to them antecedently to the issuance of a legal directive. Acknowledging the normative priority of judicial institutions Raz remarks that

> [w]hen the actions of law-creating and law-applying organs conflict, the actions of the law-applying organs are those that affect the considerations of the law's subjects: the law guides behavior by stipulating consequences that ultimately are to be *enforced* by the law-applying organs . . . According to this approach, then, the existence of the law is logically related to the practice of the law- applying organs [emphasis added].[16]

It is important to note that Raz does *not* treat coercion as a contingent feature of governance by law on the grounds that it is conceptually possible that such a system provides prudential reasons through the threat of sanctions.[17] The dimension of state coercion that he takes to be decisive for this contingent feature of law is the authorisation of coercive enforcement by a final, law-applying authority, not the backing of individual legal norms with coercive consequences. This judicial enforcement is a coercive but contingent aspect of governance by law in the sense that it purports to render more probable rather than necessitate – how could it necessitate, anyway? – people's choosing morally good options.

Judicial enforcement would not be conceptually necessary in Raz's pictur-esquely described angelic society where citizens would have a virtuous dispos-ition to live their lives under the guise of the good. But governance by law would still remain necessary because angelic beings are not also godlike and omniscient about matters of right and wrong. Angelic agents would still need legal guidance as to which type of behaviour conforms with rightful conduct

---

[16] Joseph Raz, *The Identity of Legal Systems*, 59 CALIF. L. REV. 795, 803–04 (1971).

[17] Raz explicitly rejects the autonomous legal relevance of sanction-based prudential reasons when he remarks that they are merely 'auxiliary partial reasons'. They are not legally relevant because the complete reason is not the sanction-backed norm but 'the agent's desire to avoid the sanction or the fact that it is against his interests for it to be applied to him', JOSEPH RAZ, PRACTICAL REASON AND NORMS 161 (2d ed. 1999). Moreover, they are auxiliary in the sense that '[t]hey are a most important way of securing social co-ordination and of providing people with reasons for conforming to law'. *Id.* Such complete prudential reasons must be kept distinct from the liberal-perfectionist ideal that imbues exercises of legal authority with normative relevance.

and relations, but it would be entirely pointless to additionally equip courts with coercive accessories for ensuring compliance.[18] Such angelic citizens would always be motivated to comply with what a legal authority would take to be legally required.[19]

The axiological perspective from which the contingency of the coercive character of law-applying institutions is assessed is distinctly liberal-perfectionist.[20] It is both liberal and perfectionist because mechanisms of legal enforcement treat individual autonomy (liberty) not as an end in itself but as a valuable instrument for leading a worthwhile life (perfection). Accordingly, autonomy loses its value if its exercise amounts to choosing morally bad options and it is the role of the law and other social institutions to see to it that autonomy is regularly used in a good-promoting way. Raz makes this point when he remarks that 'since our concern for autonomy is a concern to enable people to have a good life it furnishes us with reason to secure that autonomy which could be valuable. Providing, preserving or protecting bad options does not enable one to enjoy valuable autonomy'.[21]

An intermediate position between prudentially serving the interests of the sovereign and the authoritative promotion of a liberal-perfectionist ideal is occupied by Scott Shapiro's account of the 'moral aim' of law. According to this view, the fundamental aim of legal activity is to rectify by way of large-scale social planning the moral deficiencies which obtain whenever

---

[18] For a thorough and scholastically refined understanding of the contemporary importance of the 'society of angels thought experiment', see Miotto, *supra* note 6, at 277.

[19] RAZ, *supra* note 17, at 159. Hans Oberdiek defends a similar view when he notes that

> no society, human or angelic, *would* have a legal system were there no disputes and *could* have one were all disputes impossible to regulate ... Even a society of thoroughly conscientious men would find in law a useful tool for regulating their (highly principled) disputes, as well as useful in promoting opportunities and praiseworthy goals. We would, I think, recognize their system as a legal system, though it might well be free of sanctions and coercion. Hans Oberdiek, *The Role of Sanctions and Coercion in Understanding Law and Legal Systems*, 21 AM. J. JURIS. 71, 93 (1976).

[20] Kara Woodbury-Smith applies the same perfectionist axiological perspective to draw a necessitarian rather than contingentist conclusion about the coerciveness of law. According to Woodbury-Smith it is a conceptual necessity that law is coercion-apt in the sense that, even if a legal system never chooses to manifest its disposition to use coercive means, that does not mean that it is not disposed to do so if properly triggered. *See* Kara Woodbury-Smith, *The Nature of Law and Potential Coercion*, 33 RATIO JURIS 223, especially 234 (2020). For a similar view, see Leslie Green, *The Forces of Law: Duty, Coercion and Power*, 29 RATIO JURIS 164 (2016). Lucas Miotto resists the necessity of this conceptual argument by taking legal coerciveness to be a *doxastic* rather than dispositional fact. It is the availability, among other conditions, of citizens' *beliefs about* the disposition of a legal system to enforce its mandates that matters for whether law is contingently or necessarily coercive. The holding of such beliefs, then, is obviously a contingent matter. *See* Lucas Miotto, *What Makes Law Coercive When It Is Coercive*, 2 ARCHIV FÜR RECHTS- UND SOZIALPHILOSOPHIE 235, 244–46 (2021).

[21] JOSEPH RAZ, THE MORALITY OF FREEDOM 412 (1986).

a community has numerous and serious moral problems whose solutions are complex, contentious or arbitrary. The operative perspective is that of representing law as serving this general morally remedial aim. Shapiro notes that '[t]he law possesses the aim that it does because high-ranking officials *represent* the practice as having a moral aim or aims' [emphasis added].[22]

It is within this axiological context that what Shapiro describes as the 'self-certifying' coercive power of a legal system 'to enforce its rules without first demonstrating to a superior (if one exists) that its rules are valid' is a necessary aspect of governance by law in the sense that the attainment of this moral aim necessarily rests on the holding of this type of power.[23] What is jurisprudentially critical for the necessary role of coercion in law, according to Shapiro, is not the threat of sanctions but the possession of a de facto coercive power. Shapiro willingly admits the possibility of a sanctionless legal system, that is, a system that does not attach specific sanctions to its legal norms. But even such a sanctionless legal system *must* still vest its high-ranked officials with the power of self-certification on pain of ceasing to count as a legal system.[24]

This approach differs in an important way from Raz's account of the contingently instrumental role of the coercive actions of law-applying institutions. For Raz, the judicial recourse to coercive enforcement is individuated as an exercise of legitimate *authority*, whereas, for Shapiro, the necessary possession of the power of self-certification is not licensed by a supreme planning authority but by the *norms* of instrumental rationality that exist and apply independently of institutional fiat.[25]

## 1.2 The Deontic Perspective

The competing approach to the perspectival evaluation of claims about the jurisprudential status of coercion takes coercion to be a necessary or contingent aspect of the deontic character of law. Regardless of their degree of normative robustness, variations of this perspective ascribe to law construed as a system of

---

[22] Scott Shapiro, Legality 216–17 (2011). In a different context, David Plunkett remarks that, on pain of letting the planning theory of law collapse into a theory of moral planning, Shapiro must be committed to the view that the relation between legal officials and the activity of legal planning is representational in the sense that the former represent the latter as serving a moral purpose. *See* David Plunkett, *Legal Positivism and the Moral Aim Thesis*, 33 Oxford J. Legal Stud. 563 (2013).

[23] Shapiro at 221.    [24] *Id.* at 169–70.

[25] Shapiro treats the norms of instrumental rationality as explanatorily prior to legal authority when he explains that '[l]egal officials have the power to adopt the shared plan that sets out these fundamental rules by virtue of the norms of instrumental rationality. Since these norms that confer the rational power to plan are not themselves plans, they have not been created by any other authority. They exist simply in virtue of being rationally valid principles.' *Id.* at 181.

norms, mode of authority or type of political association the property of being a source of duties and rights.

The most morally detached variant of this perspective is Hans Kelsen's deontic viewpoint of the *legal scientist* who echoically presupposes the bindingness of a system's 'Basic Norm' (*Grundnorm*) in making statements about when to impute liability to sanctions. When uttering a statement of legal obligation, the 'legal scientist' – as opposed to the legal official – merely 'echoes' the normative aspiration of a legal system by expressing her disassociation from the question of whether the fact that the law requires that $\phi$ is necessarily or essentially a reason to $\phi$.[26] In Kelsen's words, '[t]he Pure Theory of Law seeks to free the conceptual characterization of the law from this ideological element [i.e., political morality] by completely severing the concept of the legal norm from its source, the concept of a moral norm, and by securing the autonomy of the law even vis-à-vis the moral law'.[27]

Kelsen devises the formal deontic perspective of treating law as a source of autonomous obligating normativity that is 'purified' – hence, his pure theory of law – from moral commitments in order to render permissible the inference of a legal normative power to impose sanctions on law subjects. It is this logically inferred normative power of imputation (*Zurechnung*) that becomes a logically necessary feature of governance by law in the sense that the logical inference of the existence of the power of imputation from the deontic perspective of the legal scientist normatively *explains* why the violation of *any* legal norm – regardless of its content – will ultimately provide a reason for the imputation to a legal subject of a liability to the imposition of sanctions.[28]

By contrast with Kelsen's detached, formal deontic perspective, H. L. A. Hart associates the jurisprudentially contingent character of coercion with the importance of the deontic perspective of committed legal officials who treat a system's rule of recognition as a source of 'common public standards' used to 'assess the *rights and duties* of particular persons by reference to the primary rules of a system or to assess the validity of any of its rules by reference to its

---

[26] As Robyn Carston explains, 'a representation is used echoically when it reports what someone else has said or thought and expresses an attitude to it'. Robyn Carston, *Metalinguistic Negation and Echoic Use*, 25 J. Pragmat. 309, 332 (1996). For the original use of the term 'echoic mention', see Dan Sperber & Deirdre Wilson, *Irony and the Use–Mention Distinction*, *in* Radical Pragmatics 295 (Peter Cole ed., 1981).

[27] Hans Kelsen, Introduction to the Problems of Legal Theory 23 (Bonnie Paulson & Stanley L. Paulson trans., Clarendon Press 1934) (1997).

[28] For a detailed exegesis of the relationship between the imputability of legal sanctions and the Basic Norm (*Grundnorm*), see Jan Sieckmann, *Kelsen on Natural Law and Legal Science, in* Kelsenian Legal Science and the Nature of Law 257, 261–66 (Peter Langford, Ian Bryan & John McGarry eds., 2017).

rules of recognition' [emphasis added].[29] It is from within this deontic perspective that the availability of a mechanism of coercive enforcement is portrayed as a contingent feature of governance by law. The coercive facilitation of deontic assessments of rights and duties rests on natural contingencies including facts like resource scarcity and the fallible, selfish behaviour of humans. For Hart, truths about the jurisprudential importance of coercion belong to a category of statements whose truth 'is contingent on human beings and the world they live in retaining the salient characteristics which they have'.[30]

It bears noting that H. L. A. Hart's famous elucidation of the role of threatened sanctions in the gunman situation is *not* meant as a direct explanation of the jurisprudential importance of coercion, but as an explanation of the normative force of legal norms. Conversely, what is made relevant as a contingent aspect of the deontic character of law is *not* the threat of sanctions attached to specific norms but the existence of a mechanism of coercive enforcement. This mechanism is relevant because and to the extent that coercively upholding law's general efficacy construed as *general obedience* can aid legal officials in continuing to meaningfully invoke the system's rule of recognition as a normative reason for validating and applying primary rules. Such general obedience, Hart clarifies,

> is not a criterion of validity provided by the rule of recognition of a legal system but is presupposed though not explicitly stated whenever a rule of the system is identified as a valid rule of the system by reference to its criteria of validity, and unless the system is in general efficacious, *no meaningful statement of validity* can be made' [emphasis added].[31]

For Hart, then, the availability of coercive means for securing general obedience – and not the attachment of sanctions to legal norms – is a contingent aspect of governance by law in the sense that it enables the reason-giving force of a system's fundamental rules when and because these rules apply to 'beings constituted as men are'.[32] For Hart, sanctions do not have jurisprudential importance in virtue of their status as prudential motives for individual compliance but in virtue of their inclusion in an organised system of enforceable *guarantees* 'that those who would voluntarily obey shall not be sacrificed to those who would not. To obey without this, would be to risk going to the wall.

---

[29] HART, *supra* note 1, at 104.   [30] *Id.* at 200.

[31] *Id.* at 295. It is within this context that Hart notes that legal officials must be able to '*presuppose* the truth of the external statement of fact that the system is generally efficacious. For the normal use of internal statements is in such a context of general efficacy' [emphasis in the original]. *Id.* at 104.

[32] *Id.* at 199.

Given this standing danger, what reason demands is *voluntary* co-operation in a *coercive* system' [emphasis in the original].[33]

Other variations of this perspective evoke more robust conceptions of the deontic character of law. A distinctly Kantian approach locates the jurispruden-tial – rather than purely conceptual – necessity of coercion *only* in the condition that *precedes* the establishment of a political community governed by law. Within this pre-legal or proto-legal condition, the merely provisional status or, equivalently, the deontic *impermissibility* of the pre-civil, private enforcement of individual rights necessitates the enforcement of a distinctly *legal*, uncondi-tional duty to enter and remain in a rightful condition that imposes reciprocal limits on everyone's freedom under public positive law. Besides the proto-legal role of the impermissibility of enforcement in a pre-civil condition, Kant does not treat cases of ordinary official coercion – as a means of deterrence (threat of sanctions) or retribution (civil and criminal enforcement) –as jurisprudentially distinct but as part of the very concept of holding a right. He then goes on to argue that 'one can locate the concept of right directly in the possibility of connecting universal reciprocal coercion with the freedom of everyone ... Right and authorization to use coercion therefore *mean one and the same thing*' [emphasis added].[34]

The main upshot of the conceptual entanglement of coercion and legal right is the distinction between the purely conceptual and the genuinely jurisprudential necessity of coercion. With respect to the former and as opposed to pre-civil, private coercion, instances of legally authorised coercion do not stand in need of *separate* jurisprudential scrutiny in terms of their individuation and justifica-tion. Legally authorised coercion *just is* a manifestation of the right itself. Metaphysically and normatively, remedial coercion is nothing over and above the legal rights that are forcibly upheld. The claim that remedial enforcement is conceptually necessitated by the concept of legal right is not a claim that

---

[33] *Id.* at 193.

[34] Immanuel Kant, *The Metaphysics of Morals, in* PRACTICAL PHILOSOPHY 353, 389 (Mary Gregor trans. & ed., 1996). A different variant of conceptual entailment is given by Grant Lamond. Instead of being a conceptual entailment of the possession of legal rights, Lamond argues, it is the concept of legal *authority* that entails a claim to possess the authority to use coercive means. In his words,

> [l]aw does not merely claim the right to alter its subjects' normative positions; it also claims the right to authorize the *enforcement* of these alterations. Law claims not merely normative authority but also coercive authority. It is not that legal duties are sanction-based, nor that every law must ultimately be linked to coercive measures, but that law claims the *right* to back up its directives with force. Grant Lamond, *Coercion and the Nature of Law*, 7 LEGAL THEORY 35, 55 (2001).

For structurally similar reasons, this conceptual argument deprives state coercion of any rele-vance over and above the relevance of legal authority.

complements in any informative way claims about the deontic necessity of legal rights. It is simply a paraphrase of the same claim about what makes the freedom of every individual compossible. What mobilises the use of a distinctly deontic perspective is Kant's idea about the jurisprudential necessity of enforcing the entry to a civil condition, not the post-entry enforcement of duties and rights. The deontic perspective that assigns jurisprudential necessity to providing an enforceable legal solution to the problem of the provisional, non-enforceable status of pre-civil or natural rights is the perspective that treats private inter-actions between persons as legally consequential, that is, as giving rise to entitlements to things other than their own bodily powers.[35]

Beyond this pre-civil scenario, the possibility and actual use of compulsive means has no distinct jurisprudential importance over and above the relevance of legal rights themselves. The reason is that, in the Kantian scheme, enforce-able legal remedies are treated as conceptual emanations of legal rights. In this civil condition setting, it is rights rather than their conceptually implied enforceability that are imbued with the deontic necessity that really matters. Accordingly, any separate engagement in modally flavoured debates about coercion is merely epiphenomenal and bears no distinct jurisprudential weight.

An alternative line of political argument does not treat officially authorised coercion as a merely conceptual aspect of legal rights but as a robust normative–political consequence of institutional practices that calls for *separate* political justification. This is a line of argument whose most lucid elaboration can be found in the jurisprudential writings of Ronald Dworkin.[36] According to this view, *both* the political decisions of legislatures and the subsequent actions of the courts and public administration are instances of official action-direction that, in the absence of proper justification, would be impermissible invasions of personal autonomy.

In this regard, these institutional (political and strictly legal) practices become legally relevant in the sense that they *trigger* principles of egalitarian

---

[35] Arthur Ripstein provides a systematic account of the content and scope of these legally consequential interactions. In his words,

> [t]hose entitlements fall under private right, and cover the traditional categories of Roman private law, relations of property, contract, and status, which govern rights to things, to performances by other persons, and, in special cases, rights *to* other persons. These categories provide a complete specification of independence between interacting persons, but can only be consistently enjoyed by all in a condition of public right with legislative, executive, and judicial branches. Each of these branches in turn has further powers grounded in its role in providing a rightful condition. ARTHUR RIPSTEIN, FORCE AND FREEDOM: KANT'S LEGAL AND POLITICAL PHILOSOPHY 17 (2009).

[36] For this approach, see RONALD DWORKIN, LAW'S EMPIRE 153 (1986); *see also* Nicos Stavropoulos, *The Relevance of Coercion: Some Preliminaries*, 22 RATIO JURIS. 339 (2009).

distributive and procedural justice which, if properly triggered, justify the coercive direction of the actions of individuals and thus render it, all things considered, legitimate.[37] Accordingly, the perspective used for the evaluation of judgements about when this triggering is successful is the perspective of a 'protestant', that is, critically reflective interpreter who treats the non-voluntary, associative relationship between citizens and their government as a source of special obligations and responsibilities.[38]

Finally, a contemporary articulation of the idea that coercion in the civil or law-governed condition is jurisprudentially otiose can be found in William Edmundson's deontic, rule-of-law perspective from which the coerciveness of institutional practices is assessed. In Edmundson's words,

> [i]f locating coercion in the world involves a preliminary drawing of moral baselines, then coerciveness in the justification-demanding sense can no longer be viewed as a cold and neutral descriptive attribute of the state ... The presumptive wrongness of the state and its activities can no longer be taken as given by its descriptive coerciveness. Moreover, depending upon what emerges as the best theory of moral baselines, it may turn out that the rule of law is not coercive, and thus not *pro tanto* wrongful.[39]

Accordingly, Edmundson sees no metaphysically compelling reason to distinguish coercively necessitated actions from naturally necessitated actions or functions, including the environmental and bodily limitations we experience as well as our needs for things such as nourishment, shelter and physical integrity. Against the background of such modes of necessitation, law is portrayed as advancing our *libertas a necessitate* (freedom from necessity) as arguably the criminal law does. If properly drafted and morally wholesome laws protect us from private violence while allowing us to act in morally permissible ways, then, Edmundson argues, the legal mobilisation of coercive means merely regularises or renders rationally expectable the mode of human responses to necessities that govern our lives independently of the law.

---

[37] For the notion of legal relevance, see Section 2.4.

[38] It is worth stressing the informative contrast with the Kantian perspective that assigns a central role not to the relationship between citizens and their rulers but to the interactions between private persons in the non-ideal context of a pre-civil condition. Dworkin, on the other hand, begins his argument *in media res*, so to speak, in the sense that he asks the question about the jurisprudential importance of state coercion once a political relationship between citizens and their government has *already* been established in one way or another.

[39] W.A. Edmundson, *Coercion, in* The Routledge Companion to Philosophy of Law 451, 460 (Andrei Marmor ed., 2012). *See also* William A. Edmundson, *Is Law Coercive*, 1 Legal Theory 81 (1995).

## 2 Changing the Question

Despite occasional revivals or reconstructions of older trends, twentieth-century analytic jurisprudence was not the jurisprudence of 'legal' coercion but the jurisprudence of legal normativity. The basic question was whether and why law is normative in any sense and coercion seemed to be a complication or distraction rather than an accessory to this explanation. It was seen as a distraction because coercion is itself a normative phenomenon that goes well beyond the operation of the state and legal systems and adheres to its own, distinct criteria of individuation.[40] Consequently, any attempt to provide a foundational account of legal normativity would be doomed to reduction if no principled way existed for keeping the two phenomena visibly apart.

In the second decade of the twenty-first century, scholarship on the jurisprudential importance of coercion has attained an unsurpassed level of sophistication and refinement in comparison with its volatile trajectory in the previous century. Numerous articles have been written and a handful of agenda-setting monographs have been published on a topic that two decades ago was still considered to be on the fringe of jurisprudential scrutiny.[41] In Section 1, I attempted to contribute to the taxonomic segment of this burgeoning scholarship. The taxonomic model sketched and updated there is not the first and definitely not the most exegetically or doctrinally comprehensive inspection of competing views on the jurisprudential importance of coercion. Other, more or less recent, accounts of the modal status of coercion in law have been defended with admirable precision and sophistication.[42]

---

[40] For the normative distinctness of coercion, see Mitchell Berman, *The Normative Function of Coercion Claims*, 8 Legal Theory 46 (2002).

[41] Among the most prominent monographs on coercion in analytic legal philosophy, the following feature: Kenneth Einar Himma, Coercion and the Nature of Law (2020); Frederick Schauer, The Force Of Law (2015); and Ripstein, *supra* note 35.

[42] Without hesitation I would instantly single out as exceptionally illuminating Lucas Miotto's consecutive contributions to the taxonomic and conceptual quest of making sense of the way legal philosophers of diverse jurisprudential allegiances make sense of the necessity or contingency of coercion in law. Miotto is a contingentist about the role of coercion in law but his approach to making sense of the modality of law's coercive operation is motivated by premises that do not presuppose anything robustly committing about this modality. Miotto's approach is highly refined in the sense that it takes the relation between law and coercion to be asymmetrical in a variety of flavours (ontological, epistemic, analytical, conceptual and pragmatic). His model of relations of dependence by law and coercion is further refined by allowing different specifications of legality to figure as a relatum. Instead of simply talking about law and coercion, Miotto suggests that we should be more specific and 'discuss instead, for example, whether legal obligation, or legal authority, or legal systems, or the content of law, or whatever depends (in a given sense) on coercion. This means that for each of these five understandings of the dependence relation there will be several distinct theses to be discussed.' Lucas Miotto, *Law and Coercion: Some Clarification* 34 Ratio Juris. 74, 75 (2021). *See also* Miotto, *supra* note 6 and Miotto, *supra* note 20.

In this section, I will provisionally digress from the taxonomic quest. I say 'provisionally' because in the next and final section I will resume the taxonomic mode of my exposition, but by this time I hope to have shifted the context in which I will be juxtaposing some major theories about the jurisprudential importance of coercion. To shift the context in which we consider competing theories of coercion we need to change the question we care to ask in relation to law and coercion. This is precisely the task I will try to deliver in this section, and it is only through this task that I dare to consider a novel contribution to the existing literature. My preceding attempt at devising my own taxonomic model for representing different jurisprudential answers to the modal question of whether law is necessarily or contingently coercive was not original in any substantial sense. If it can withstand further scrutiny by peer taxonomists, it will eventually remain one among other supplementary, overlapping or competing alternatives for making sense of this division of opinion.

My aspiration for originality is limited to only one sense and this sense is not taxonomic but metaphysical. Driven by some metaphysical concerns that I will spell out further downstream, I will replace the *modal* question of whether governance by law is necessarily or contingently coercive with what I will label the *metric* question of how (much) legally inexorable state coercion is. For a thorough explanation of how this replacement will work, I will need to fill in more detail as to how I understand the notion of *inexorability*. As soon as this notion has been adequately elucidated, more will be said about the merits and reasons for resisting the modal question.

The first step is to bring greater precision to the sloganesque claim that we should care to know how (much) legally inexorable state coercion is. Inexorability is not a direct attribute of situations involving state coercion but of the *truth* of propositions about the legal relevance of such situations. A detailed account of how I plan to use *legal relevance* as a term of art will have to wait until Section 2.4. As I also very briefly mentioned in the Introduction, the general idea is that legal relevance is a way of being legally normative. This normativity is not only the normativity of reason-giving. To say that truths (true propositions) about the legal relevance of state coercion are inexorable is to say that they hold in an especially secure or unshakeable way. So, a more complete formulation of the metric question would be:

*How (much) inexorable are truths about the legal relevance of situations of state coercion?*

Different theories can settle this metric question in different ways. Inexorability will be treated as a gradable property of truths (true propositions) about the legal relevance of state coercion and, consequently, disagreements about the degree of this inexorability will be metric disagreements. One theory may hold that truths about the legal relevance of state coercion are inexorable to the highest degree, whereas another theory may hold that truths about the legal relevance of state coercion are not inexorable at all. In the last case, if the slightest variation in how the world is configured is enough to falsify the proposition that state coercion is legally relevant, then the truth of this proposition is very fragile.

A basic intuition about necessary propositions such as 'necessarily, governance by law is coercive' rests on the idea that the truth of this claim remains inexorable or secure despite variations in the context of its assertion or, in metaphysical terms, despite the obtaining of counterfactual situations that exert pressure on the preservation of its truth. This dimension of inexorability is often expressed by way of asking ourselves how difficult it would be for the proposition that state coercion is legally relevant in this way or that way to fail to be true. The more difficult it is for something to fail to be the case, the more inexorable the truth of a statement about it will be. By analogy, the more difficult it is for the proposition that a situation of state coercion is legally relevant in a certain way to fail to be true, the more inexorable or secure is its truth.

This metric question about the legal relevance of state coercion is meant to be original only in its focus, not in its conception. It is a faithful application of Boris Kment's radically original and hence potentially controversial metaphysical account of modality. It bears noting that none of Kment's pioneering views is part of the picture of modality that we inherited from Kripke, and only one of them, the claim about the reducibility of modal concepts to non-modal concepts, is found in David Lewis's alternative picture.[43] Kment sets the aim of explaining necessity in terms of truth security. His metaphysical account is motivated by a compelling intuition about the nature of modal thought and talk. In his words,

> modal thinking is intimately connected to a very common cognitive routine: reflection on how great a departure from actuality is required for the realiza-tion of a certain scenario. English has a sizable inventory of phrases that allow us to express beliefs about this. Many of them (though not all) use the metaphors of distance or security. For example, we say that something was a close call, or that Fred nearly won the race, got very close to being promoted, or got within a hair's breadth of disaster, to communicate that various situations are close to actuality. The peace between two nations during some period in history can be called fragile or secure, depending on how easily their tensions could have escalated into war.[44]

---

[43] David Lewis, Counterfactuals 52–56 and 118–42 (rev. ed. 2001).
[44] Boris Kment, Modality and Explanatory Reasoning 30 (2014).

Kment's security and my inexorability are notional equivalents. The reason I opted for the latter term is that security carries with it some distinctly legal connotations that would distract us from the metaphysical orientation of the argument. Accordingly, alethic inexorability or, in Kment's terms, alethic security, is a dimension or metric 'on which true propositions can occupy different positions, and that to be metaphysically necessary *is simply to have no less than a certain value on that scale*' [emphasis added].[45] This is to say that, in our case, truths about the legal relevance of situations involving state coercion can be of varying degrees of inexorability; but, for the sake of simplicity, I will arbitrarily single out four regions on this scale. I will be assigning to the propositions held to be true by different theories the highest, moderate, minimal or zero degree of inexorability. In the latter case truths about the legal relevance of state coercion will only hold in the context of present or historical legal systems as they are presently or were historically configured.

More generally then, for any true proposition $P$, how easily $P$ could have failed to be true depends on how great a departure from actuality is required for $P$ not to be true. The greater the departure required, the more secure is $P$'s truth. Boris Kment provides a concise explanation of the connection between necessity as inexorability or security and the concept of closeness to actuality. He writes,

> the kind of security of truth that we talk about when we say that a proposition couldn't have been false (i.e., that it is necessary) relates to how easily that proposition could have been false. Moreover ... how easily a proposition could have been false is determined by how much we need to depart from actuality to get to a world where the proposition doesn't hold: the greater the departure required, the less easily the proposition could have failed to be true.[46]

Accordingly, the more difficult it is for a proposition about the legal relevance of state coercion to fail to be true the more inexorable its truth will be. Difficulty of falsification is the ultimate measure of coercion's jurisprudential inexorability. The degree of difficulty for a truth about the legal relevance of state coercion to fail to be true will depend on the range of situations *alternative to what we treat as the actuality of governance by law* in which this proposition *remains* true. If a jurisprudential proposition about the legal relevance of state coercion remains true only in situations that depart just minimally from the actuality of a law-governed world, then we could say that the truth of this proposition is very fragile. As I will explain in Sections 2.1 and 2.2 below, I will further specify the typical actuality of a law-governed world by reference to what I will henceforth

---

[45] *Id.* at 28.    [46] *Id.* at 29.

be calling 'lawmaking facts'. The actual legal world, in other words, will be narrowly construed as the world configured by how law is made.

Settling the metric question will involve a 'metaphysical' kind of measurement. The degree of inexorability of a true proposition about the legal relevance of state coercion can be measured by measuring the distance between what a particular theory of law treats as the actual legal world – which, as said, I will define as the world where law is made – to the closest alternative worlds in which the proposition is false. The modal status of state coercion for a system of governance by law becomes a metric matter of the degree of inexorability of truths about state coercion rather than a categorical matter of necessity or possibility: a theory of law will portray governance by law as *coercive to a higher degree* the greater the distance from the legal actuality of lawmaking it allows for the proposition that state coercion is legally relevant to *remain true*. The degree of coerciveness assigned by a given theory to governance by law is determined by this comparison. The more inexorable the truth about the legal relevance of state coercion, the more coercive governance by law is believed to be.

Providing this more committed view on how the notion of alethic (truth) inexorability can be used to re-articulate the jurisprudential discussion about the coercive character of governance by law is only the very first step in a series of necessary concessions, additions and clarifications. Nothing said so far merits a shift of jurisprudential focus as pronounced as I ventured to make at the beginning of this section. In the remainder of Section 2, I will divide the issues raised by this shift of focus into tightly composed subsections for the purpose of facilitating the reader in deciding which of the premises of my advertised 'metric question' marks the greatest departure from the modal articulation of this debate.

The issues I have singled out correspond to the basic premises of my argument in favour of replacing the modal with the metric question. These are: (a) my understanding of legal actuality as the point of departure from which we measure the degree of inexorability of truths about the legal relevance of state coercion; (b) my narrow emphasis on the state and its coercive practices; (c) the notion of lawmaking facts or situations; and (d) the notion of legal relevance.

## 2.1 Legal Actuality

Replacing the modal question of whether governance by law is necessarily or contingently coercive with a metric question resides in the possibility of manipulating, so to speak, some jurisprudentially important variables. By tweaking these variables, we can make interesting measurements and comparisons both with respect to particular theories and, most importantly, with respect to how two or more theories come to disagree on the matter. Because the metric question takes the inexorability of truths about the legal relevance of state coercion to be a matter of degree, it needs to posit a point from which the determination or measurement of degrees of such inexorable truths is made. Variations in degrees of inexorability will be treated as variations in the distance from a jurisprudentially privileged description of the actuality of governance by law that is required for a proposition about the legal relevance of state coercion to remain true. The greater the distance from this actuality *where truth is preserved* the greater the degree of this truth's inexorability.

A very plausible worry about the way the metric approach understands the requisite measurement is that it is not intelligible at all to treat governance by law *as a whole* or, equivalently, a typical legal system in its totality, as the point of legal actuality from which we commence our measurement of how inexorably true the legal relevance of state coercion is.[47] The reason is that, on pain of begging the question of whether governance by law *is* coercive, we cannot assume that the reality (actuality) of such a comprehensive type of governance can be wholly described in a way that makes no reference to coercive practices as part of its actual operation. Put more succinctly, for scenarios of legally relevant state coercion to be jurisprudentially informative, any departure from actual legal situations needs to differ *in precisely the sense that the latter are not coercive as such* whereas the former are coercive and yet remain true for all jurisprudential purposes.[48]

---

[47] Lucas Miotto also takes typicality to be an important parameter in determining the jurisprudential importance of coercion. He remarks that '[t]ypical legal systems satisfy the coerciveness conditions in a typical way; they satisfy such conditions in virtue of displaying particular features and facts. In fact, one could even think – perhaps rightly – that part of the reason why a legal system is typical is that it satisfies the coerciveness conditions in a typical way.' Miotto, *supra* note 20, at 239. My use of the expression 'typically legal' is very different from Miotto's. I define legal typicality in terms of legal actuality and, most importantly, I further define legal actuality in terms of the reality of how law is typically made. So, for the purposes of my argument, legal typicality just is the reality of how law is typically made. Miotto reserves a much more familiar understanding for the same expression. He takes typicality to be a direct attribute of a legal system. On his construal, typical legal systems are 'legal systems made by humans to address human needs'. Miotto, *supra* note 6, at 278. In another article he also adds that he will 'take "typical legal systems" to refer to those legal systems that currently exist in western democratic states and those that closely resemble them'. Lucas Miotto, *The Good, the Bad, and the Puzzled: Coercion and Compliance*, in Conceptual Jurisprudence: Methodological Issues, Conceptual Tools, and New Approaches 111, 112 (Jorge Fabra-Zamora & Gonzalo Villa Rosas eds., 2021).

[48] Of course, this is not to say that coercive laws – that is, laws backed up by the threat of sanctions – cannot be *made* coercive or that laws *thus and so made* are not judicially or administratively enforceable! They are made coercive but they are not made *coercively* although they are coercive or enforceable. The latter concerns the content and the application of the law, respectively, not the creation of law. At any rate, and even if we assume the radical legal sociological view that

Departures are differences and the differences that matter in our discussion are differences between coercive and non-coercive ways of configuring the law. They are not differences between more coercive and less coercive scenarios of governance by law, nor between one way in which governance by law can be coercive and other ways in which the same type of governance can be coercive. Propositions about legally relevant scenarios of state coercion are evaluated for the degree of inexorability of their truth with respect to how much the context in which these situations obtain can differ from a non-coercively defined legal actuality *without failing to obtain as legally relevant*. They remain legally relevant *despite* the fact that, by virtue of certain criteria that need to be specified, the context of their obtaining is determined in a way that is very different from the way the reality of governance by law is determined.

This brings me to what I believe is the most crucial and perhaps weakest premise in my entire argument. The metric approach will be as frail as this premise, and this is a possibility I cannot exclude. I will assume that, for the sake of representing the tenacity of truths about the legal relevance of state coercion, we can narrow the actuality of governance by law to what I believe we can treat as its most basic aspect, namely, the typical avenues for creating law and its surrounding context. The metaphysical avenue through which law is made makes no essential *metaphysical* reference to coercion, and yet interesting comparisons of the Kmentian type I just described can still be made because *both* lawmaking and official coercion can be assessed by reference to the same dimensions.[49] The first dimension is the perspectival dimension we encountered in Section 1. It is composed of two halves, an axiological half and a deontic half. The second, ontological dimension will be introduced in the next section and will be composed of a normative half and a descriptive half. Of lawmaking and state

---

there can exist legal systems where the *making of law* is nothing over and above the coercive direction of particular actions by the particularised edicts of *Rex*, I remain confident that I still have most analytic legal philosophers on my side when I suppose that lawmaking involves the creation of something general and that *this* generality cannot be metaphysically accounted for by the way coercion or potential coercion works. H.L.A. Hart would be the last one, I think, to abandon my side. In his mention of a legally primitive or sub-legal type of governance, he writes,

> on this account of the social situation under Rex, the habit of obedience is a personal relationship between each subject and Rex: each regularly does what Rex orders him, among others, to do. It is to be observed that in this very simple situation all that is required from the community to constitute Rex the sovereign are the personal acts of obedience on the part of the population. HART, *supra* note 1, at 52.

[49] I emphasise 'metaphysical' because there are jurisprudential theories that make essential normative–political reference to facts about coercion in their account of how law is made. Dworkin's law as integrity is one such theory. Dworkin's interpretivist theory is a special case for the additional reason that it resists the relevance of robustly metaphysical or 'Archimedean' theoretical viewpoints on the nature or normativity of law.

coercion we can equally ask: (a) which perspective applies for evaluating the truth of propositions about their legal relevance; and (b) are lawmaking practices and acts, or practices of official coercion, individuated descriptively or normatively?

Legal actuality will be equated with the reality of how law is typically made, and this reality will be the privileged point of departure from which all comparisons will be made. Typicality in my account will be radically theory-sensitive. It is not empirical, statistical, inductive or historical typicality. It is the typicality that a given jurisprudential theory takes to be the generic (typical) avenue for making law.[50] Truths about the legal relevance of state coercion will be more inexorable, secure or unshakeable *the more different or distant the context in which they still obtain is from the context in which propositions about the legal relevance of lawmaking facts are held to true by a given jurisprudential theory.*

My proposal can resist critical pressure, I believe, if one is willing to accept, or concede for the sake of argument, that the most metaphysically basic aspect of a system of governance by law is the reality that emerges from the way in which law is created. All other layers of legal reality – including, most prominently, the application and enforcement of law – are grounded in the reality of lawmaking. For law to be applied and enforced it first needs to be made into law. Assuming, as I just did, that this level of governance by law is the most metaphysically basic licenses us, I believe, to treat it as the narrow but fundamental ingredient of what I have been referring to as typically legal actuality.

An informative metric assessment will now be possible. Truths about the way in which state coercion is legally relevant will be more inexorable the more different or distant the context in which they still obtain is from the context in which propositions about how facts about the making of law are legally relevant are true. The two comparable truths will be truths about the legal relevance of state coercion and truths about the legal relevance of lawmaking facts. The dimensions of similarity or difference between these two truths will be provided by the two dimensions of the taxonomic model I will present and apply in Section 3.

---

[50] Another important difference between my account and Lucas Miotto's account is that he seems to draw a sharper line between 'the debate about the extent to which typical legal systems are coercive, and the debate about whether legal systems are necessarily coercive'. Miotto, *supra* note 20, at 239. The latter debate is the debate to which the modal question directly applies. My metric question aims to fuse these two debates into one by allowing the notion of actuality to become a *comparandum* for judgements of jurisprudentially relevant similarities and differences between itself and situations involving state coercion. Only relevant similarities and differences matter and what is relevant is a function of what is typical of the existence of the two *comparanda*: state coercion and lawmaking. Relevant similarities cannot be similarities between atypical instances of either state coercion or lawmaking.

## 2.2 Lawmaking Facts

Prosaically put, lawmaking facts are facts about the generation of law from non-law. They are facts about the creation, generation or production of law. A more jurisprudentially refined definition that can replace this awkward expression is that a lawmaking fact is a fact about *how* the property of legal validity is conferred to something that is not intrinsically legal. The property of legal validity need not be cashed out in metaphysically robust terms. Different theories assign varying metaphysical weight to this notion, hence deflationary approaches are also possible. In what follows, I will be flagging some correlations between different accounts of legal validity and my talk of facts about how legal validity is conferred. My emphasis on the 'how' of validity conferral is meant to flag the importance of distinguishing reportative or verdictive facts about something's being legally valid – that is, '$X$ has the property of being legally valid in system S' – and facts whose obtaining *makes it the case* that legal validity is instantiated by something capable of bearing it. Only the latter facts are lawmaking facts.

Lawmaking facts are facts that convey a story about the *creation* of the bearers of legal validity or, equivalently, the *way* in which legal validity has come to be acquired, not about the bearing of legal validity per se. This bearer can be an abstract object, an event or a property instance, depending on a theory's jurisprudential commitments. All three types of entity are amenable to individuation by recourse to certain metaphysical criteria. As is the case in all types of constructive or building metaphysical relations, the objects, events or properties that are made into law are not intrinsically legal. They *become* legal by virtue of a lawmaking fact.[51] Something whose criteria of individuation are not legal in an essential sense comes to acquire the property of being legally valid when and because certain jurisgenerative conditions obtain that enable the conferral of this property. Facts about the operation of these jurisgenerative conditions are our lawmaking facts. Consider the following three statements of fact:

*Object*: *O* constitutes (has the status of) a *legal* artefact.
*Event*: A process culminates in a *legal E*.
*Property instance*: *P* is a *legal* manifestation of (namely, a legally relevant effect of exercising) a power.

To say that an abstract 'artefact' (constitutively) becomes legal, or that an event (processually) becomes legal or that a property instance (dispositionally) becomes legal is to say that legal validity has been conferred. Each statement

---

[51] For the notion of building relations in metaphysics, see Karen Bennett, *Construction Area (No Hard Hat Required)*, 154 PHILOS. STUD. 179 (2011).

describes the obtaining of a jurisgenerative state of affairs. In other words, it describes a metaphysically distinct conception of a lawmaking fact, and each statement conveys information about how legal validity is conferred. This jurisgenerative or validity-conferring situation can amount to the obtaining of a relation of abstract constitution (*Object*), the termination of a culminating process (*Event*) or the manifestation of a power (*Property instance*). In *Object* the conferral of legal validity consists in the obtaining of a relation of abstract constitution between a lawmaking kind of 'stuff', *O*, and a law (legal artefact).[52] In *Event* the conferral of legal validity consists in the culmination of a lawmaking process into an event that is properly individuated as a legal enactment. Finally, in *Property instance* the conferral of legal validity consists in the exercise of a power in a legally proper or felicitous way.

I am fully aware that, in their present formulation, these statements barely resemble anything a layperson could or would associate with a fact about the making of law. For example, a quotidian understanding of lawmaking could be informed by the idea that lawmaking is like the execution of a recipe for making some food. Following certain steps that involve the use of certain 'materials' and the presence of certain persons arranged in a certain place (texts, seals, deputies, ballots, assembly hall etc.) and the performance of certain actions results in the making of a law or laws. Although laws are not edible, they are valid and that's what is needed to pronounce our recipe-making successful.

Ordinary reports of lawmaking facts could include statements such as 'the Parliament of country X has unanimously voted to enact a bill on social media franchises', 'the government of country Y has issued a decree on workplace hygiene' or 'Congress has made it illegal to provide material support to foreign terrorist groups'. Such statements have certain distinctive markers: they are temporally and locationally indexed (e.g., on 21 March 2022 in the capital of Calisota, Duckburg); they use juridical terms (statute, constitution, parliament, government); and they involve an agent or a group of agents, an action and a result. Ordinary language seems to be so much better equipped to meaning-fully describe truths about the properties, actions or things (artefacts) whose instantiation, performance or production respectively counts as an instance of lawmaking.

Abstractions like *Object*, *Event* and *Property instance* cannot emulate the plasticity of ordinary juridical or folk descriptions of lawmaking, but this was not the cause they purported to serve in the first place. These formulaic

---

[52] For the notion of abstract constitution, see Simon Evnine, *Constitution and qua Objects in the Ontology of Music*, 49 Br. J. Aesthet. 203 (2009).

statements reflect alternative metaphysical conceptions of lawmaking, and their language of articulation is distinctively logico–metaphysical. Despite grammatical appearances, the metaphysically primary dimension of lawmaking need not be taken to be a sort of process or activity as conveyed by *Event*. In *Event* the process of lawmaking culminates in the occurrence of particular events such as the enactment of a text, the signing of a treaty or the issuance of a decree. Leaving variations aside, such events have a prominently linguistic dimension as evidenced by the fact that they carry a certain kind of illocutionary meaning or force.[53]

Accordingly, in *Event* a lawmaking fact will be a fact about the culmination of a lawmaking process in an event that can be described as a legal enactment. In linguistic studies of the phenomenon of verbal aspect, events of this type are called telic and they constitute the major class of linguistically relevant discrete events.[54] A telic event, or achievement as it is also known, consists maximally of two distinguished sub-events, a temporally extended process (lawmaking) and an instantaneous culmination (enactment) at which a result state is reached. Some linguists describe telic events or achievements as instantaneous or durationless events in the sense that they cannot in themselves occur over or throughout a temporal stretch. An example is the sentence, 'Anita recognised Peter the moment he entered the room.' Recognition is not a temporally extended occurrence. Likewise, the moment of enacting a law can also be construed as a punctate or instantaneous 'achievement'.

An alternative view sees telic events as boundaries of eventualities or 'boundary happenings', that is, happenings that literally take place on the precipice of a change from an activity-like eventuality into a state-like eventuality. Peter's walking into the room ends at the boundary of recognition which marks the beginning of a state of objectual knowledge (Anita is in the state of knowing Peter). On this approach, the logic of achievements is the logic of beginnings and endings where the ending of something is immediately followed by the beginning of something else.[55]

Maris Köpcke provides a very detailed account of this approach. Köpcke treats legal validity as a juridical technique in the sense that 'it is common to valid things that they are made and, crucially, that they are made through

---

[53] For this view, see Nicholas Allott & Benjamin Shaer, *The Illocutionary Force of Laws*, 61 INQUIRY 1 (2017). John Searle takes the promulgation of laws to have both declarative (effective) and directive force; *see* John Searle, *A Classification of Illocutionary Acts*, 5 LANGUAGE IN SOCIETY 1, 22 (1976).

[54] *See* Robert Truswell, *Event Composition and Event Individuation, in* THE OXFORD HANDBOOK OF EVENT STRUCTURE 90 (Robert Truswell ed., 2019).

[55] *See* Christopher Piñón, *Achievements in an Event Semantics*, VII PROCEEDINGS OF SALT. 273 (1997).

a distinct kind of technique: in essence, by someone saying so'.[56] Köpcke's 'saying so' is the culmination of a lawmaking or validity-conferring process – or, in her terms, a technique – that must precede any acknowledgement that legal validity has been successfully conferred.[57] Crucially, legal validity is not exclusively attributed to enactments but also to sub-legislative entities such as wills, licences, marriages, appointments or mortgage assignments. Köpcke rejects the common view that the entities that are primarily legally valid are legal norms, rules, standards or provisions. As she explains,

> 'When the technique of validity begins to be forged, to be devised as a tool to effect far-reaching social and political transformations, validity is first and foremost a property of *acts*, chiefly of acts arranging personal relations in the sphere of private life and business, such as contracts, wills, marriages or gifts. Eventually, in the Middle Ages, validity comes to be predicated, by extension, of particular official acts such as appointments or judgments, until, around 200 years ago, it starts to gain currency as a property of *general* enactments and their abstracted products, legal norms – once, that is, juristic consciousness has embraced the possibility that even the legislature's say-so may be legally constrained by a legally binding body of constitutional law. In an important sense, focus on valid norms and their criteria of validity is an offshoot, perhaps a creature, of modern constitutionalism [emphasis in the original].[58]

Alternatively, lawmaking can also be understood as being primarily about the exercise of some kind of power. This power need not be identical with legislative power or with legal authority, namely, the power to impose legal duties and rights. These are only some among many available jurisprudential options. Other types of power whose exercise can be taken to have a lawmaking effect are the power to obtain justification for using the collective force of the state, the power to rule over a sovereign territory, the power to will something as a law (legislative will) or, perhaps most controversially, the power to improve the moral situation – this is a plausible rendition of Mark Greenberg's view[59] – or the power to compensate for the moral deficiencies of the state of nature. All these are powers and not all of them attract familiar or ordinary juridical descriptors. This is not an alarming situation

---

[56] MARIS KÖPCKE, LEGAL VALIDITY: THE FABRIC OF JUSTICE 3 (2019).

[57] Alternatively, the culmination of a lawmaking process can be individuated as legal if, for instance, certain constitutive conventions apply with respect to when the termination of a lawmaking activity acquires the label of legality. On the role of constitutive conventions in lawmaking, see ANDREI MARMOR, *Constitutive Conventions, in* POSITIVE LAW AND OBJECTIVE VALUES 1–24 (2001).

[58] *Id.* at 7–8.

[59] In a footnote to 'The Moral Impact Theory of Law', Greenberg acknowledges the strong connection between the notion of the legally proper way of changing the moral profile and the normative capacity (power) of proper legal systems to improve the moral situation. *See* Mark Greenberg, *The Moral Impact Theory of Law*, 123 YALE L.J. 1288, 1324 (2014).

because jurisprudential theories of diverse commitments (natural law, positivism, interpretivism etc.) will vest their description of lawmaking powers with their preferred ontological cloak, so to speak. Accordingly, *Property instance* as well as *Object* and *Event* are metaphysical abstractions, not paraphrases of familiar juridical or jurisprudential expressions. Their language is ontologese not legalese.

In *Property instance* the exercise of such powers will result in the instantiation of certain properties – some metaphysicians would call them 'tropes' – that can be attributed to the agent(s) who exercised this power. These properties will be as diverse and fine-grained as the powers to which they are attached. Depending on one's jurisprudential allegiances, the property can be ascribed to the individual, collective or aggregated intentions of an agent(s) or to the legal system as a normative kind. In *Property instance* a lawmaking fact will be a fact about the legally felicitous or proper way that a power is manifested.

For instance, legislative intention is such a property instance that can be associated with exercising the power of legal authority in a validity-conferring way. To use Joseph Raz's theory as an example, the intention with which a legal official exercises her lawmaking power is identified as legally proper if 'it is, or is at least presented as, someone's view of how its subjects ought to behave [and if it can be identifiably ascribed to] the alleged authority without relying on reasons or considerations on which [the] directive purports to adjudicate'.[60] Conversely, non-positivistically inclined theorists may take the public's understanding of the effect of exercises of legislative power rather than the legislature's actual intentions to be the most relevant mental property instance.[61]

Even more radically, the relevant property instance might be the *legally proper moral effect or impact* of exercises of the power of a 'genuinely binding' legal system to improve the moral situation. This power is patently more abstract than any ordinary, positivistically defined lawmaking power and exercises of this more abstract power are individuated as the actions, not the intentions, of legal institutions. Abstracting somewhat from Mark Greenberg's original formulation of this novel view, moral impact can be understood as any change in what Greenberg calls the *moral profile* of a political society that is the result of the actions of lawmaking institutions. A political society's moral profile is the set of 'all of the moral obligations, powers, permissions, privileges, and so on that obtain in that society'.[62]

---

[60] Joseph Raz, *Authority, Law, and Morality*, in Ethics in the Public Domain: Essays in the Morality of Law and Politics 210, 218 (rev. ed. 1994).

[61] *See* Hillel Levin, *Contemporary Meaning and Expectations in Statutory Interpretation*, 2012 U. Ill. L. Rev. 1103 (2012).

[62] Mark Greenberg, *The Standard Picture and Its Discontents*, in Oxford Studies in Philosophy of Law, Vol. 1 39, 56 (Leslie Green & Brian Leiter eds., 2011) .

Accordingly, there obtains a chain of morally interconnected property instances which, if legally felicitous, terminates in what Greenberg calls 'legally proper moral changes'.[63] Exercises or manifestations of a legal system's power to improve the moral situation are institutional actions, and actions are properties of institutional agents, collective or individual. To these actions are attributable certain morally relevant changes. These moral changes, in turn, are properties of a political society's moral profile and *facts about the manifestation of a legal system's power to improve the moral situation by these property instances* are a 'Greenbergian' type of lawmaking fact.

Finally, in *Object* a lawmaking fact is treated as a fact that tells a story about how an abstract acquires the property of being legally valid. Being perhaps the most ordinary view among contemporary legal positivists, the artefactual view takes the bearers of legal validity to be abstract objects like norms, rules, provisions or, more prosaically, laws. Hans Kelsen is an archetypical proponent of this view. Kelsen claimed that validity is 'the specific existence of norms' and that these norms stand in a mereological relation to a legal system as a whole.[64] This latter remark partly overlaps with H. L. A. Hart's understanding of legal validity, chiefly as a rule's membership in a system of law. 'To say that a given rule is valid', Hart writes, 'is to recognize it as passing all the tests provided by the rule of recognition and so as a rule of the system'.[65] Joseph Raz chimes in when he notes that '[a] rule which is not legally valid is not a legal rule at all'.[66]

In more metaphysically graphical language, the same story can be narrated by the statement that facts about the making of law are like facts about the execution of a 'recipe'. It is a fact about what type of lawmaking *stuff* or material constitutes a law or, in metaphysically proper terms, a legal artefact. Lawmaking, here, is neither a culminating process nor a manifestable power but literally, albeit awkwardly, a kind of stuff-like ingredient necessary for 'cooking' something into law. Accordingly, assertions of lawmaking facts are assertions of which pre-legal stuff constitutes legal objects (norms, rules, plans etc.) and, as such, they perfectly qualify for being labelled as recipe-making or, in more formal language, claims of abstract constitution. This kind of recipe-making represents a moment of creation, so to speak – it is as though we are told: take some substance $S$ and add some structure to it and you will get a piece of law. The conferral of legal validity

---

[63] Greenberg, *supra* note 59, at 1321–22.

[64] HANS KELSEN, GENERAL THEORY OF LAW AND STATE 30 (A. Wedberg trans., 1945). In the same vein, see HANS KELSEN, GENERAL THEORY OF NORMS 28 (M. Hartney trans., 1991). For a critical analysis of this view, see Dick W.P. Ruiter, *Legal Validity qua Specific Mode of Existence*, 16 LAW AND PHILOSOPHY 479 (1997).

[65] HART, *supra* note 1, at 103.

[66] JOSEPH RAZ, THE AUTHORITY OF LAW: ESSAYS ON LAW AND MORALITY 146 (1979).

amounts to the obtaining of such a relation of abstract constitution. Claims about the constitution of abstract artefacts like musical or literary works can be equally represented as carrying recipe-like information.

While it remains controversial whether some abstract artefacts (like musical works) can literally be created rather than mentally discovered or tracked, constitutive talk is no less frequent in aesthetic discourse. For instance, on Jerrold Levinson's modest account of musical Platonism, a musical work is constituted by a sound-structure-as-indicated-by-x-at-y.[67] By analogy, a jurisprudential variant of this view could be that a legal artefact is constituted by a *text-type-as-indicated-by-x-at-y*. Alternatively, an artefact could be individuated as legal if it is actually or counterfactually represented or intended as serving a particular function.[68]

## 2.3 Stateless Coercion

The third clarification is with regard to the empirical scope of my argument. The modal question of whether governance by law is necessarily coercive is articulated in such a way that no essential mention need be made of the state, its apparatuses and its practices. Moreover, the modal question takes coercion to be a modally potent property of governance by law, while the comparison licensed by the metric question takes the state to be the principal vehicle of coercive action. Consequently, one could plausibly retort that the metric approach is either a more specific or, worse, a biased variant of the more general modal question.

It is more specific because it talks about state coercion while excluding the coercive dimension of institutional practices taking place at the international, transnational or peripheral level. Such practices are not centrally organised, but

---

[67] Jerrold Levinson, *What a Musical Work Is*, 77 J. PHILOS. 5 (1980).

[68] Roman Ingarden develops the idea that public artefacts are partly individuated by what is considered as a proper instance of their use. He notes, '[w]ith a piece of cloth, for example, we clean pots. To the flag we render military honors; we preserve it, often for centuries, as a remembrance, even though the cloth of the flag is badly damaged and without any value.' ROMAN INGARDEN, THE ONTOLOGY OF THE WORK OF ART 260 (1989). In a similar vein, Amie Thomasson suggests that

what seems most basic in many cases is the intention that the creation be subject to certain norms, in the sense that it be recognizable as something that is to be treated, used, or regarded, in some ways rather than others ... It is the intended normative features (that the object be subject to certain norms) that drive the intended recognitional features ... as well as many intended structural features. Amie Thomasson, *Public Artifacts, Intentions and Norms*, in ARTEFACT KINDS: ONTOLOGY AND THE HUMAN-MADE WORLD 45, 52 (Pieter Vermaas et al. eds., 2014).

In the jurisprudential literature, Kenneth Ehrenberg maintains that '[l]aws are artifacts in that they are specialized creations of human intentionality that serve specific purposes and are designed in order to be recognized as such'. KENNETH EHRENBERG, THE FUNCTIONS OF LAW 175 (2016).

they are nonetheless coercive and law-like. Why should truths about the legal relevance of state coercion be the exemplary case whose degree of inexorability we care to measure? Why not also try to measure the degree of inexorability of truths about the legal relevance of *stateless* coercion? This is an interesting question that would merit inclusion in an essay whose topic presupposes an affirmative answer to the question of whether an international (like the United Nations) or peripheral (like the European Union) normative order is also a typical legal system, or, in my preferred terms, a system of governance by law that can be taken to have an incipient or sui generis form of lawmaking function.[69]

Without the dimension of lawmaking, the metric approach cannot provide an informative answer to the question of how inexorably true are propositions about the legal relevance of stateless coercion. Inexorability is a gradable property, and its measurement relies on measuring a certain type of difference on a certain scale. The *comparanda* that the metric approach takes to be the objects of this measurement are the contexts in which situations of state coercion remain legally relevant in a certain way and the contexts in which situations about the making of law are legally relevant in a certain way. While lawmaking can be reasonably taken to be the most fundamental function of a municipal legal system from which all other functions derive their legal importance, it certainly cannot be taken to be a basic function of an international normative order. The absence of an international legislative process has also been one of the main reasons why H. L. A. Hart preserved his doubt as to whether international normative orders are also legal systems in a metaphysically robust sense.[70]

For these reasons and perhaps for a host of other reasons that evade me at the moment, the metric question I have just placed on the pedestal of this inquiry may appear as lacking the doctrinal pedigree or philosophical generality for accommodating concerns about the coercive nature of international normative

---

[69] Most legal scholars would agree that the European Union *is* a typical legal system, albeit of a supranational type, that obviously has a lawmaking function by virtue of which directives and regulations are issued. European Union legislation is proposed by the European Commission and approved by the Council of the European Union and the European Parliament to become law. What the available textual space allows me to note here is that, although there is broad consensus that the European Union is a legal system with a proper lawmaking capacity, its enforcement mechanisms and, to some extent, the juridical incorporation of the 'products' of its lawmaking procedures are essentially mediated by the institutional resources of member states. Consequently, if we are interested in measuring the degree of inexorability of propositions about the coerciveness of the European Union as a system of supranational governance, we will need to determine the legal relevance of facts about EU coercion and, perhaps also, the legal relevance of facts about the making of EU law in a way that essentially registers facts about the coercive and lawmaking practices of member states.

[70] *See* Hart, *supra* note 29, at 3–4, 214. For a critical analysis of Hart's reserved account of the legal-systemic character of international law, see Mehrdad Payandeh, *The Concept of International Law in the Jurisprudence of H.L.A. Hart*, 21 Eur. J. Int. Law 967 (2011).

orders.[71] This is a valid concern that I cannot mute but only mitigate by remarking that, as soon as we switch to the comparative mode, a different dimension of coercion becomes visible, namely, that, no matter what else is true of them, coercive practices are an undeniable feature of the state. Whether they are also an undeniable feature of the law is a real question that different theories will have different reasons to settle. So, if we really care to know whether governance by law is really coercive, which better avenue than to devise a principled way to compare a dimension of this type of governance with the most typically coercive institution that the world's political history has offered so far.

My point is that as soon as we switch from the modal mode of thinking to the comparative mode it becomes much harder to continue to feel the urge to make informative inferences about the nature of governance by law from examples of stateless mechanisms or supranational avenues for the collective use of force. The reason is that the metric question is not systematically ambiguous as the modal question is between two sub-questions, namely, the question about the coercive character of laws (legal norms) and the question about the coercive character of legal systems. The metric question takes the metaphysically committing step of articulating the problem of coercion in law at the level of a *system* of governance by law instead of at the level of individual legal norms or rules. Accordingly, for someone like me, who feels the urge to replace the modal question with the metric question and also wants to remain charitably agnostic about the metaphysics of supranational normative orders, there is no remaining motivation to try to equip the metric approach with the tools necessary for measuring the degree of inexorability of truths about the legal relevance of *stateless* coercion.

## 2.4 Legal Relevance

Painting with a broad brush, I would like to propose a fairly neutral description of how I intend to use the notion of legal relevance further downstream. First, for reasons of proper regimentation, I will treat legal relevance as a property of

---

[71] For an original view of how the international law practice of 'outcasting' can be seen as the primary avenue of international law enforcement, see SCOTT SHAPIRO & OONA HATHAWAY, THE INTERNATIONALISTS: AND THEIR PLAN TO OUTLAW WAR (2017). The authors argue that

> [i]n place of war, international law relies on outcasting. The 1969 Vienna Convention on the Law of Treaties, which is a treaty about treaties, states that ... if a state fails to follow a treaty, the states that are affected can refuse to follow it as well. Ironically, international lawyers refer to this peaceful form of retaliation by a military term: 'countermeasures'. Countermeasures must be proportional to the harm done by the original breach. Countermeasures must also be productive, not punitive. The goal is not vengeance, but rather to bring the bad actor back into line. *Id.* at 376.

facts rather than a property of actions. I shall presume that the type of facts or situations to which legal relevance can be attached are *non-legal* facts in the very narrow sense that they are not facts about the existence of *legal facts* or facts about the content of the law, that is, facts about the obtaining of general legal obligations and rights, or alternatively, facts about the existence of legal norms. This condition is strict enough to classify as non-legal, for the purposes of my argument, the two types of fact that will occupy the slots of the taxonomic exercise I will resume in Section 3, namely, facts about state coercion and lawmaking facts.

The first type of fact that I plan to consider is in regard to instances of *state coercion* broadly construed. Such 'coercive' facts can be institutional facts about the statutory codification and judicial or administrative imposition of sanctions; facts about the existence, performance and operation of a mechanism for enforcing penalties and other sanctions; facts about the regulation and the actual use of physical compulsion by authorised officers; or facts about the execution of particularised orders. The second type of fact regards instances of *lawmaking*. Lawmaking facts are neither identical with legal facts, that is, facts about the existence of legal norms or facts about the obtaining of legal obligations, rights or powers, nor with verdictive facts about which norms are legally valid. In Section 2.2 I provided an adequately detailed account of how facts about the *way* in which legal validity is conferred can play the role of lawmaking facts.

Moreover, and before I get into further detail about the notion of legal relevance, I should flag an important limitation on the inclusiveness of the notion of legal relevance. Lawmaking facts can never be legally relevant in the trivial sense of being relevant *for the making of law*. Legal relevance is not *jurisgenerative* relevance. For the purposes of my argument legal relevance will stand for the *more specific ways* in which coercion-involving or lawmaking-involving facts display, manifest or exemplify *legal normativity*. Legal normativity is a species of practical normativity along with moral, prudential, political and, perhaps, aesthetic normativity. It need not be confined to the normativity of reasons for action as the recent trend in metaethics suggests.

Evaluative concepts like good or bad, aretaic concepts like virtuous or vicious, thick evaluative concepts like courageous or cruel as well as other deontic concepts such as fittingness[72] and rightness[73] are equally normative

---

[72] *See* Richard Rowland, *Reasons or Fittingness First?*, 128 Ethics 212 (2017); Richard Yetter Chappell, *Fittingness: The Sole Normative Primitive*, 62 Philosophical Quarterly 684 (2012).

[73] Laura Schroeter & François Schroeter, *Reasons as right-makers*, 12 Philos. Explor. 279 (2009).

notions. Whether these notions can be reduced to the notion of a reason is a fervent and still unsettled metaethical question whose pending resolution does not vitiate the use of these concepts in a taxonomic model that is not about their relation. Accordingly, legal normativity will be construed in a way that is broad enough to accommodate robust, reductionist and deflationary as well as deontic, evaluative and aretaic approaches. Different jurisprudential theories may diverge to a greater or lesser extent with respect to how they construe the normative nature or function of law.

It also bears noting that, properly speaking, it is lawmaking facts and not *legal facts* that can be legally relevant in the sense of exhibiting a certain mode of legal normativity. Legal facts are facts about the existence of legal norms or the obtaining of legal obligations and rights. From a metanormative point of view these facts are what Jonathan Dancy calls 'verdictive' or 'conclusory': they make true, either alone or in conjunction with other verdictive moral facts, reports about how the question of whether or not to $\varphi$ has been settled.[74] They are practical verdicts about whether $\varphi$-*ing* is or is not to be done. They do not also provide a further normative reason to $\varphi$ on top of the reasons that justify or explain the verdict or conclusion. Legal facts are legally verdictive but not legally relevant in the technical sense I have reserved for this term here.[75]

In the remainder of this section, I will supplement with an adequate number of jurisprudentially diverse examples a trichotomy of modes of legal relevance.[76] In defence of the trichotomy's general scope of application, the examples I will mention will feature cases of legally relevant facts about state coercion *as well as* lawmaking facts. The trichotomy captures three dimensions that can be normatively qualified: the dimension of borne normativity, the

---

[74] The term 'verdictive' was originally introduced by Philippa Foot; *see* Philippa Foot, Virtues and Vices 181 (2003). Arguing for the verdictive character of facts about moral rightness, Jonathan Dancy notes that 'it is incoherent, in this light, to suppose that the rightness can add to the reasons on which judgment is passed, thus, as one might say, increasing the sense in which, or the degree to which, it is true'. Jonathan Dancy, *Should We Pass the Buck?*, 47 Royal Inst. Phil. Supp. 159, 166 (2000). Dancy insists that if a verdict were allowed to count as a reason for itself, 'we would be forced to reconsider the balance of reasons once we had asserted [the verdict] in a way which would continue ad infinitum. Which is ridiculous'; *see* Jonathan Dancy, Ethics Without Principles 40 (2004).

[75] For an excellent advocacy of this view in the case of legal facts, see Christopher Essert, *Legal Obligation and Reasons*, 19 Legal Theory 63 (2013). For the opposite view that legal facts can be legally relevant in the reason-giving sense, see Kenneth Einar Himma, *The Ties that Bind: An Analysis of the Concept of Obligation* 26 Ratio Juris. 16 (2013) and Noam Gur, *Legal Facts and Reasons for Action: Between Deflationary and Robust Conceptions of Law's Reason-Giving Capacity, in* The Normative Force of the Factual: Legal Philosophy Between is and Ought 151 (Nicoletta Bersier Ladavac, Christoph Bezemek & Frederick Schauer eds., 2019).

[76] For a metaethical analysis of the general notion of normative relevance, see Pekka Väyrynen, *Grounding and Normative Explanation*, 87 Proc. Aristot. Soc. Suppl. Vol. 155 (2013).

dimension of normative explanation and the dimension of normative modification. Each type of dimension will be associated with examples from the domain of coercive institutional practices as well as the domain of what makes law.

A last point of caution regarding the use of this trichotomy is that I will not focus exclusively on the normative guidance or constraint of either civilian or official behaviour. *Both* civilian and official conduct are significant aspects of legal normativity, and both can be associated with the legal relevance of facts about official coercion and lawmaking. Where the focus lies is a matter of jurisprudential theory, or sometimes, ideology. Legal officials need not be the recipients of official coercion in order to be normatively guided or constrained by certain facts about the way this coercion is operationalised. For instance, legal interpretivist theories take facts about state coercion to play a distinct normative role in the judicial determination of the content of enforceable legal rights and duties. In such cases, the reasons provided by facts about the coercive record of past government actions are primarily reasons for official enforcement consistent with a certain scheme of principle rather than reasons for civilian action.[77]

With these preliminaries we can move on to the slots made available by the so-called trichotomy of legal relevance. The first type of legal relevance concerns cases where a certain fact bears a certain kind of *normativity*. The respective normative status may derive its force from diverse sources of normativity such as law – if treated as autonomously normative – morality, prudence or rationality. This is consonant with the possibility that for some jurisprudential theories legal normativity *just is* moral or prudential normativity. Depending on a theory's jurisprudential commitments, this can be the normativity of providing a distinctly legal or moral reason for compliance with legal duty, the normativity of providing a prudential reason for conformity with a legal norm, the normativity of operating as a rational constraint on combinations of law-directed attitudes or the normativity of being instrumental to the attainment of an end that is good or is represented as being good in a certain respect.[78] Relative examples can be gleaned from various levels of abstraction

---

[77] Dworkin clearly associates the normativity of the coercive practices of the state with their bearing on the content of enforceable claims of right or obligation. This association is accompanied by a distinction between the institutional reasons for principled enforcement provided by these practices and the reasons for action provided by the fact about the obtaining of a political obligation, namely, a general moral obligation to obey the law. Dworkin frames this distinction as being between the problem of the legitimacy of coercive power and the problem of political obligation. *See* DWORKIN, *supra* note 36.

[78] To say that A is instrumental to the attainment of B is to say that A-ing is a *way of* B-ing. There are at least three ways of being a means for something. A-ing can be a *part* of B-ing (as when dissolving yeast is part of baking bread), or brutely constitutive of B-ing (as, in the relevant context, when raising my hand counts as bidding on a horse at auction) or, finally, a species of

where facts about lawmaking practices or official coercion are subject to jurisprudential evaluation.

For instance, it could be argued that the coercion-related fact that a right holder is definitively assured of a coercively enforceable remedy provides a legal reason to enforce this remedy on demand. In a similar vein, we may say that the lawmaking fact that an exercise of the power of legal authority results in the issuance of an authoritative directive provides a legal reason to act to the exclusion of competing non-legal considerations; or that the fact that the lawmaking power of a legal system is manifested when the voting of a statutory text has created legitimate expectations as to what should be done provides a legal reason to validate that expectation by acting as the statute requires.[79] From the viewpoint of a sanction-centred theory, the same fact that an exercise of the power of legal authority has resulted in the issuance of an authoritative directive can also serve as a prudential reason to comply for the sake of avoiding the imposition of sanctions.

Joseph Raz's theory of law attributes a different, rationalistic mode of legal relevance to lawmaking facts about the exercise of the power of legal authority. Lawmaking facts about the exercise of legal authority are legally relevant in the sense that they bear the normativity of providing a content-independent reason to intend to act as the authoritative pronouncement dictates, or, equivalently, to treat the pronouncement as settling the question of what to do.[80] An entirely different flavour is attached to the normativity borne by 'lawmaking plans'.[81] Scott Shapiro's plan positivism maintains that the lawmaking fact is not a fact about the exercise of legal authority, but rather a fact about the exercise of rational planning power whose legitimation relies exclusively on the principles of instrumental rationality. The fact that the exercise of this rational power has resulted in the formation of a plan, *P*, that is believed to be a means for

---

B-ing (as when swimming becomes a species of physical exercise). Accordingly, a legal institutional action of the coercive or lawmaking sort can be legally relevant in virtue of its being a way of realising a valuable state of affairs. For this distinction, see Candace Vogler, *Nothing Added: Intention §§19 and 20*, 90 AM. CATHOL. PHILOS. Q. 229, 230 (2016).

[79] For the role of public expectations and their relation to democratic considerations, see Hillel Y. Levin, *Contemporary Meaning and Expectations in Statutory Interpretation*, 2012, 1103 U. ILL. L. REV. (2012).

[80] Although Joseph Raz's jurisprudential prose frequently suppresses the utility of the distinction between reasons for action and reasons for intention, there are occasions where he recognises that authoritative guidance is a source of reasons to *deliberate* in a way that assigns normative priority to the edicts of an authority. Raz expresses this idea when he notes that '[a]uthorities tell us *what to intend*, with the aim of achieving whatever goals they pursue through commanding our will' [emphasis added]. JOSEPH RAZ, *The Problem of Authority: Revisiting the Service Conception, in* BETWEEN AUTHORITY AND INTERPRETATION: ON THE THEORY OF LAW AND PRACTICAL REASON 126, 135 (2009).

[81] By 'lawmaking plans' I mean lawmaking facts about the exercise of planning authority, namely, the authority or power to plan for others.

implementing the system's *Master Plan*, *M*, is legally relevant in the sense that it gives rise to a rational requirement to intend to fulfil, monitor and readjust *P* if the legal officials of that system treat *M* as morally legitimate. The normativity of this rational constraint is rather weak in the sense that it does not directly provide a compelling legal or prudential reason to intend the ensuing steps, but only to avoid the state of affairs where legal officials treat the system's master plan as morally legitimate *without also* intending to implement it through more concrete planning.

Another way for a fact about state coercion to be legally relevant is to serve as the *explanatory ground* of whichever normativity (distinctly legal, moral, prudential or rational) another fact bears. For instance, an interpretivist can argue that facts about the principled judicial enforcement of past political decisions figure in the grounding explanation of why the enactment of a statute provides a reason for the present enforcement on demand of an affected right or responsibility. Conversely, a sanction-based theory of law would license the rephrasing of the previous statement in the service of its own premises about how sanctions are legally relevant. For instance, it could be argued that the fact that it is likely that the sovereign will carry out a threat to X if someone does not Y grounds the fact that a sovereign imperative provides a prudential reason to conform with the edicts of a sovereign authority.

On the lawmaking side, a moral impact theorist can argue that the lawmaking fact that a legally proper change in a society's moral profile is the result of the exercise of a legal system's normative power to improve the moral situation is legally relevant in a normative-explanatory sense. In other words, it figures in the right-making explanation of why certain law-compliant actions are right as well as why certain law-violating actions are wrong. According to Mark Greenberg's account, whenever law is made, there should be a change in facts about what is the right thing to do because, in his view, exercises of the power of legal institutions to improve the moral situation are legally relevant precisely when and because they operate as right-making facts.[82]

Finally, a third way in which facts can be deemed as legally relevant is by virtue of their operating either as *background conditions* or as *modifiers of the normative weight* of other 'coercive' or lawmaking facts which provide legal or merely prudential reasons for action.[83] For example, one may argue that the

---

[82] '[T]he explanation of what makes an action right or wrong ... strikes me as the closest analogy in the moral domain to the explanation we're concerned with in the legal case.' Mark Greenberg, *Explaining Legal Facts*, UCLA School of Law Research Paper No. 08–19, 4 (Aug. 2007), https://ssrn.com/abstract=1139135.

[83] For a formal account of this mode of normative relevance, see Ralf Bader, *Conditions, Modifiers, and Holism, in* WEIGHING REASONS 27–55 (Errol Lord & Barry Maguire eds., 2016).

coercion-related fact that there exists an effective mechanism for maintaining security and punishing wrongdoers enables the enactment of a criminal statute to change the morally relevant circumstances in a way that makes it legally impermissible to use violence.[84] From a pragmatic perspective, a counterpart statement about the same fact could be that the coercion-related fact that there exists an effective mechanism for maintaining security and punishing wrong-doers enables the enactment of a criminal statute to dissuade scofflaws from acting contrary to the edicts of a legal authority.

Ronald Dworkin's interpretivist theory of law is also an example of how lawmaking facts are legally relevant in this conditioning sense. Dworkinian lawmaking facts are facts about the culmination of certain institutional practices into enactments or, more broadly, political decisions.[85] According to Dworkin, facts about such culminated processes become legally relevant when and because they trigger or enable the application of principles of distributive and procedural justice.[86] Principles of the first type govern the distribution of the benefits and burdens of living in a politically organised society. Principles of the second type govern the deliberative processes by which legal institutions decide to shape rights and obligations in a particular way.

Legal doctrine is also rich in examples of cases where the legal relevance of certain institutional facts consists in, for instance, attenuating the normative weight of a lawmaking fact. On one possible understanding of the normative force of appellate decisions, it can be argued that a statute found repugnant on grounds of its incompatibility with a charter of human rights provides *less* reason for subjects to take or refrain from a relevant course of action. In such cases there is room for arguing that the fact about the rights-incompatibility of a statutory provision attenuates the normative weight provided by the fact that a particular statute has been enacted. In doing so, it prevents the statute from providing an otherwise decisive reason for action.[87]

---

[84] Mark Greenberg makes a suggestion along these lines; *see* Greenberg, *supra* note 59, at 1311.

[85] Nicos Stavropoulos alludes to Dworkin's processual/eventive understanding of lawmaking when he notes that 'Institutional practice is conceived in terms of actions and attitudes, not norms or communication of norms. We start at what people do and say and think. Assemblies draft, debate, amend, and enact statutes.' Nicos Stavropoulos, *Legal Interpretivism*, The Stanford Encyclopedia of Philosophy (Edward N. Zalta ed., Spring 2021 Edition), https://plato.stanford.edu/archives/spr2021/entries/law-interpretivist/.

[86] For a political account of facts about state coercion as a trigger of egalitarian distributive principles, see also Gabriel Wollner, *Equality and the Significance of Coercion*, 42 J. Soc. Philos. 363 (2011).

[87] For an elaboration of this instance of legal relevance, see Hrafn Asgeirsson, *Can Legal Practice Adjudicate Between Theories of Vagueness?*, *in* Vagueness and the Law: Philosophical and Legal Perspectives 95, 106 (Geert Keil & Ralt Poscher eds., 2016).

## 3 Testing the New Question

In the previous section I set out to do what I had postponed in Section 1 of this Element. Having sketched the contours of a taxonomic model that could represent modal claims about the jurisprudential importance of coercion, I conditionally withdrew my endorsement. The condition I introduced in the previous section is not in regard to the taxonomic model itself but the question it purports to represent, and I tried to infuse the context of this new question with some content. What I have done is to offer some good reason in favour of tolerating the replacement of the modal articulation of claims about law and coercion with the metric articulation. This is a preliminary requirement to which the remaining exposition is answerable.

The metric question can be a worthwhile methodological alternative to the more traditional modal question only if it can still address a central metaphysical issue that *also* preoccupies a great portion of modal thought and talk. This issue has to do with whether and to what degree the world freely varies or comes to differ from how it is actually configured. Modal discourse certainly cares about the freedom of worldly variation or differentiation even though it resists the idea that this is ultimately a matter of gradation in the amount of some normative or descriptive magnitude. It is often assumed that necessity and possibility are all-all-nothing matters and the gradability of difference from how things actually are is not a typical feature of a modal description of the world.[88]

For lack of reckonable expertise in modal metaphysics, I will not challenge this intuition even though others who are real experts have done so.[89] What I want to retain from this discussion is that, among the other things that modal thought and talk cares about, it also cares about variations in worldly states of affairs. These variations are measurable and because they are measurable, they come in degrees. This is the narrow but central metaphysical issue I intend to use as the bridge that makes my departure from the modal to the metric question smoother than perhaps initially thought.

---

[88] Recent work on modality in formal semantics has highlighted the fact that many modal expressions are gradable. For example, they accept at least some degree modifiers and can take part in comparatives and equatives. *See* Daniel Lassiter, *Graded Modality*, in THE WILEY BLACKWELL COMPANION TO SEMANTICS (D. Gutzmann et al. eds., 2021), https://doi.org/10.1002/9781118788516.sem074; Seth Yalcin, *Epistemic modals*, 116 MIND 983 (2007); Seth Yalcin, *Probability Operators*, 5 PHILOSOPHY COMPASS 916 (2010); PAUL PORTNER, MODALITY (2009).

[89] *See*, again, KMENT, *supra* note 44. For a nomic analysis of modality, see Matthew Tugby, *The Laws of Modality*, 179 PHILOS. STUD. 2597 (2022). For a critical review of Kment's theory, see Nina Emery & Christopher S. Hill, *Impossible Worlds and Metaphysical Explanation: Comments on Kment's Modality and Explanatory Reasoning*, 77 ANALYSIS 134 (2017).

As I just explained, the metric question takes the issue of variations from the actual world as seriously as the modal question does. But as happens with all replacements, it also takes at face value something that the modal question suppresses or paraphrases, namely, the idea that the worldly difference is not a categorical, either/or matter but a matter of degree. A situation can differ from the way the world is actually configured *to a greater or lesser degree*. Let us provisionally shoulder the metaphysical commitment that these abstract entities we call situations are *states* or *conditions*, of varying detail and complexity, that a concrete world is in. These situations are *ways* that things, as a whole, are. Let us also assume that there are or are likely to be *different* ways that things as a whole are and that things as a whole can be different to a greater or lesser degree from an initial configuration or arrangement. *Difference or similarity in the ways* a world is configured will be the scale on which we can measure the inexorability of certain truths about the legal relevance of state coercion. One way may be more or less different than the actual or typical way of truthfully assembling a world together. The more different one way of truthfully reassembling the world from the actual or typical way, the more inexorable the truth about this reconfiguration will be.

In this last section I will try to explain in the terms licensed by the metric question the varying degrees of inexorability that competing theories attribute to the truth of their judgements about what makes state coercion legally relevant. If all goes well, the take-home lesson from this explanation will be that shifting the question about law and coercion in this way equips the taxonomic model with an additional virtue: its capacity to weed out instances of verbal jurisprudential disagreement about the coerciveness of law. The latter capacity is not about the classification of competing jurisprudential theories of coercion. It is about the conditions under which theories occupying different slots or quadrants – as I will be calling them in this taxonomy can be contrasted and adjudicated.

Such contrasts will be informative and meaningful if the theories contrasted can agree on a common answer to a question that *precedes* the asking of the metric question, namely, *by which criteria do we assess the legal relevance of lawmaking facts*. This is because, by the lights of this new approach, the meaningfulness of the modal disagreement over the coerciveness of governance by law is reduced to the meaningfulness of a *metric* disagreement over the obtaining of a gradable alethic property: the inexorability of truths about the legal relevance of state coercion. Such truths will be more inexorable the more different the context in which they obtain is from the context in which certain truths about how law is made hold.

If two theories apply different criteria for determining the context in which certain lawmaking facts acquire their legal relevance, there will be no common point from which competing measurements can take place. If the parties apply different criteria for determining the legal relevance of *both comparanda*, then they have not yet embarked on a joint project of comparison. Comparison is always posterior to a non-comparative act or judgement of determination. The context in which we assess the truth of propositions about the legal relevance of one of the two comparanda needs to be determined by a set of criteria before moving on to the actual comparison. Jurisprudential disagreement has a temporal or ordinal structure because its subject matter is, to put it lyrically, the collective progressive writing of a story.

The remainder of this section will be divided in three sub-sections. In Section 3.1, I will introduce the second ontological dimension, which, along with the familiar perspectival dimension, will compose a two-dimensional model that I will use to test the new, metric question on two pairs of jurisprudential theories. The perspectival (axiological–deontic) and ontological (normative–descriptive) dimensions will provide the criteria of similarity and difference between the actuality of how law is made and scenarios involving state coercion.

In Section 3.2, I will explain the order of weight between different kinds of relevant similarities. More precisely, ontological similarities between the actuality of how law is made and scenarios involving state coercion will be weightier than perspectival similarities between the same types of situation.

In Section 3.3, I will test the metric question by contrastively examining two pairs of jurisprudential theories. These theories are Joseph Raz's authority-based variant of exclusive positivism (theory A), Ronald Dworkin's legal interpretivism (theory B) and Arthur Ripstein's Kantian theory of law (theory C). The first pair featuring theories A (Raz) and C (Kant) will provide an instance of substantive disagreement about the degree of jurisprudential importance of state coercion, whereas the second pair featuring B (Dworkin) and C (Kant) will provide an instance of verbal disagreement over the same issue.

## 3.1 The Second Axis

In the service of widening the scope of the model, I would like to introduce the second axis that provides a separate standard for individuating lawmaking practices, as well coercive actions and practices, in an ontological sense. In developing this two-dimensional taxonomy, I have benefitted immensely from Scott Anderson's two-dimensional proposal for classifying competing theories of coercion as a general rather than a narrowly jurisprudential phenomenon. Anderson has written extensively on how to operationalise the hypothesis that 'accounts of coercion can be mapped onto two different axes: whether they focus on the situation of the coercee or the activities of the coercer; and whether or not they depend upon moral judgments in their analysis of coercion'.[90] Moreover, and very importantly for the inclusiveness of my own taxonomic endeavour, Anderson offers compelling arguments for reviving the distinction between what he calls two kinds of coercion, namely, the case of physical compulsion or force and the dispositional case of action- or response-inducing pressure.[91] Anderson refers to the former kind as the subject matter of a distinct approach to coercion which he calls the 'enforce- ment approach'.[92]

My two-dimensional taxonomy is different in some important respects. First, it 'normativises' the coercer–coercee axis by transforming it into an axis that features two opposing practical perspectives for the truth-evaluation of modal or normative propositions that can be further specified in a variety of dimen- sional halves. Anderson's *coercer* corresponds to my general *axiological* per- spective. Anderson's *coercee* corresponds to my general *deontic* perspective. Second, it 'ontologises' the moral–non-moral baseline axis. Both halves of the latter axis play an ontological role in the sense that they figure in the ontological explanation of what individuates acts or practices as coercive.

The overarching question about the ontology of coercion is whether coercion is individuated in a normative or, conversely, descriptive way. This question is pitched at such a high level of abstraction that trying to answer it will include settling a series of more specific questions, such as:

(a) Are offers coercive in the same way that threats are?

(b) Does the use of physical force to manipulate another as a mere means (e.g., manipulating someone's hand to force their signature) count as an instance of coercion?

(c) Is an act coercive because of the coerciveness of its cause, its effects or both?

---

[90] Scott Anderson, *Of Theories of Coercion, Two Axes, and the Importance of the Coercer*, 5 J. Moral Philos. (2008) 394, 394.

[91] For coercee-centred accounts, see Mitchell Berman, *The Normative Function of Coercion Claims*, 8 Legal Theory 46 (2002) and H.J. McCloskey, *Coercion: Its Nature and Significance*, 18 South. J. Philos. 335 (1980). Anderson treats this distinction as a revival in the sense that recent accounts of coercion treat it almost exclusively as a dispositional concept. This modern trend is a clear departure from when '[c]ontemporary philosophical writing on coercion as a special subject [began] virtually from scratch with essays by Robert Nozick in 1969 and Harry Frankfurt in 1973, and a collection of essays on the subject in the NOMOS series, published in 1972'. S. Anderson, *How Did There Come to Be Two Kinds of Coercion?*, in Coercion and the State 17, 17–18 (David A. Reidy & Walter J. Riker eds., 2008).

[92] *See* Scott C. Anderson, *The Enforcement Approach to Coercion*, 5 J. Ethics Soc. Philos. 1 (2010).

(d) Is coercion a success concept such that the concept of 'failed coercion' is as conceptually unintelligible as 'married bachelor'?

(e) Is coercion an intrinsically normative or moral concept?

The overarching question about the ontology of lawmaking is whether legal artefacts, legal enactments or legal properties are individuated in normative or descriptive terms. More specific issues in the vicinity of this general question include topics such as:

(a) Can lawmaking practices be described in non-legal terms?

(b) Do lawmaking practices have a constitutive aim or purpose?

(c) By what criteria do lawmaking practices make a contribution to the content of the law of a certain jurisdiction?

(d) Is the creation of law metaphysically distinct from the application of law?

(e) Is the content of the law identical with the content of the mental states of lawmaking officials or the linguistic meaning of legislative texts?

All these questions presuppose in one way or another a committed view on the more general question of whether a theory of coercion or a theory of how law is made needs to posit a normative or, conversely, a descriptive baseline for distinguishing instances of coercive behaviour or jurisgenerative practices from other types of action-direction or norm-guidance, respectively.

For instance, it matters whether a particular theory uses the vocabulary of reasons and rational explanation to speak about the causes of coercive acts. Insofar as causes are treated as a species of reasons, the most natural avenue for individuating acts of coercion is normative, although not necessary moral. Appeals to reasonableness or prudential value can suffice.[93] The same concern applies to a theory's understanding of the effects or impact of coercive treatment on the coercee. Consequences can be individuated in descriptive terms (e.g., measurable psychological or neurophysiological effects) or in normative terms (e.g., effects that violate the rights of the coercee).

In a similar vein, it matters how a theory accounts for the intermediate metaphysical layer where lawmaking facts reside. This a layer that lies between the social–linguistic facts or, also – for non-positivists – more basic normative

---

[93] For the role of reasonableness as a *normative* individuating criterion, see Miotto, *supra* note 6. Miotto notes that '[d]espite the lack of agreement on the details, most philosophers accept that enforcement mechanisms are coercive only if they make non-compliance with legal mandates *unreasonable* in some non-trivial sense (to be specified by an account of coercion)' [emphasis added]. *Id.* at 296. Miotto applies this individuating criterion in a way that supports his contingentist view that 'coerciveness is not tantamount to the presence of sanctions and enforcement mechanisms and … [that] a legal system is coercive only when the enforcement mechanisms render non-compliance with legal mandates unreasonable in some non-trivial sense is all an argument for the contingency of coerciveness in legal systems needs'. *Id.*

facts and the corresponding legal facts about the existence of legal norms or the obtaining of legal obligations and rights. Ontological accounts of lawmaking facts can be robust or deflationary. What matters is that they are somehow accommodated within the framework of a jurisprudential theory.

Advocating for the latter case, Mark Greenberg suggests that it must be possible to describe lawmaking facts, or, as he prefers to call them, 'legal-content-laden facts' about what counts as a validly appointed legislature or a valid bill in entirely non-legal terms, hence without using predicates like 'legally valid', 'statute', 'constitution' and so on. At the same time, however, Greenberg resists assigning a robust explanatory role to lawmaking facts on the grounds that 'there must be more basic facts in virtue of which the legal-content facts obtain. To build legal-content facts into law practices would beg the question at the heart of this paper – the question of the necessary conditions for law practices to determine the content of the law'.[94]

The ontological axis purports to assist in addressing concerns of this kind. It does so by making available the use of two types of ontological criteria, descriptive and normative, for the individuation of coercive acts and lawmaking practices. As previously explained, the importance of action-individuation has been elaborated in great detail by Scott Anderson whose model I intend to emulate to a significant degree. Anderson's talk of moral and non-moral base-lines corresponds to my normative–descriptive ontological axis. Whereas my axis is meant to accommodate answers to all the more specific questions enumerated above, Anderson focusses only on one of them. He remarks that the baseline-based model for individuating coercive acts 'is generated by a need to distinguish threats from offers as a central criterion of coercion. Threats and offers are both proposals put to the coercee, aiming to influence her behavior, and distinguished with respect to how they affect what is normal for the coercee'.[95]

## 3.2 Closeness-Relevant Similarities and Their Weights

The representation of metric instead of modal disagreements between jurisprudential theories is made possible by measuring the comparative closeness to the actuality of legally relevant lawmaking facts of two theoretically competing

---

[94] Mark Greenberg, *How Facts Make Law*, 10 Legal Theory 157, 167–68 (2004).

[95] Scott Anderson, *Coercion*, The Stanford Encyclopedia of Philosophy (Edward N. Zalta ed., Summer 2021 Edition), https://plato.stanford.edu/archives/win2017/entries/coercion/. For a general account of the normative–descriptive divide in the individuation of coercive interactions, see Robert Nozick, *Coercion*, in Philosophy, Science, and Method: Essays in Honor of Ernest Nagel 440 (Sidney Morgenbesser, Patrick Suppes & Mary Terrell White eds., 1969).

scenarios where state coercion remains jurisprudentially important. This comparative measurement of proximity to legal actuality is made on the basis of weighing the similarities that the first coercion-related scenario has to lawmaking actuality against those that the second coercion-related scenario has to the same actuality. The perspectival and ontological dimensions or axes provide the two types of similarity that are relevant for ordering the position of a scenario about the legal relevance of state coercion in relation to the actuality of how law is made.

The first relevant similarity with respect to the actuality of how law is made is similarity in the way in which acts of state coercion and 'laws' are ontologically individuated. Depending on a given theory's ontological commitments, 'laws' can be shorthand for legal artefacts, legal events (enactments) or legal properties. Accordingly, each half of the ontological axis corresponds to two ways in which two competing scenarios can be '*individuation-similar*' to the actuality of lawmaking. That is to say, a state coercion scenario, A, can be closer than scenario B to the actuality of lawmaking if, according to the theory under review, the criteria for individuating state coercion in A, but not the criteria for individuating state coercion in B, are the same as the criteria for the individuation of 'laws'. As previously explained, depending on the theory under review these criteria can be either descriptive or normative.

The second relevant similarity with respect to the actuality of how law is made is similarity in the practical perspective from which the truth of judgements about the legal relevance of state coercion is evaluated. Each half of the perspectival axis corresponds to two ways in which two competing scenarios can be '*perspectivally similar*' to the actuality of how law is made. That is to say, a state coercion scenario, A, can be closer than scenario B to the actuality of how law is made if, according to the theory under review, the perspective on which the obtaining of A, but not the obtaining of B, is evaluated is the same as the perspective according to which the truth of propositions about the legal relevance of lawmaking facts is evaluated.

Besides the two axes of similarity between scenarios about the legal relevance of state coercion and the actuality of how law is made, the model offers a principled way of ordering the comparative closeness of competing scenarios on the basis of their relative weights. To cite a familiar motto, 'ontology comes first'. This is to say that, among the two similarity dimensions mentioned, similarities in the ontological criteria for individuating instances of state coercion or lawmaking are the weightiest. Consequently, the second weightiest criterion will be coincidence in the (choice of) standards for evaluating the truth of claims about legal relevance. This ordering becomes visible in the example illustrated in Figure 1.

*Philosophy of Law*

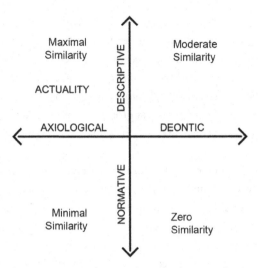

**Figure 1** An illustrative commensuration of state coercion and lawmaking

Figure 1 depicts the ordering of similarity between scenarios of state coercion and the actuality of how law is made which is hypothetically located in the upper-left quadrant (descriptive–axiological). Assuming, for the sake of argument, that a given theory takes 'laws' to be descriptively individuated and the truth evaluation of judgements about the legal relevance of lawmaking facts to be based on an axiological perspective, the similarity of competing scenarios about state coercion to this actuality will be estimated on the basis of the quadrant in which our example theory takes its licensed situation to reside. Accordingly, the following four possibilities emerge:

(1) *Maximal similarity to lawmaking actuality*: state coercion is individuated on the same grounds as the individuation of 'laws' *and* the judgement about the legal relevance of state coercion is true relative to the same perspective as that invoked for the evaluation of the truth of judgements about the legal relevance of lawmaking facts. In this case, state coercion turns out to be a trivial aspect of law precisely because our example theory makes it impossible to configure legally relevant situations of state coercion within the parameters of a quadrant other than the quadrant of legal actuality. In this case, the degree of inexorability of the truth of a proposition about the legal relevance of situations of state coercion is *zero*. By the lights of such a theory, the falsifiability of propositions about the legal relevance of situations of state coercion is extremely easy relative to legal actuality. The easier the falsification, the lesser (down to zero) the degree of inexorability.

(2) *Moderate similarity to lawmaking actuality*: the grounds for individuating state coercion are the same as the grounds for the individuation of 'laws' *but* the judgement about the legal relevance of situations of state coercion is true relative to a perspective (deontic) that differs from the one that assigns truth to judgements about the legal relevance of lawmaking facts (axiological perspective). In this case, the inexorability of the truth of a proposition about the legal relevance of situations of state coercion is of a relatively *moderate* degree.

(3) *Minimal similarity to lawmaking actuality*: the judgement about the legal relevance of situations of state coercion is true relative to the same perspective as that invoked for the evaluation of the truth of judgements about the legal relevance of lawmaking facts (axiological perspective) *but* the grounds for individuating state coercion are different (normative) from the grounds for the individuation of 'laws' (descriptive). In this case, the inexorability of the truth of a proposition about the legal relevance of situations of state coercion is of a relatively *high* degree.

(4) *Zero similarity to lawmaking actuality*: *both* the individuation of situations of state coercion and the justification of their legal relevance depends on different standards (normative grounds and deontic perspective) from those that a given theory applies to the individuation of 'laws' and the determination of the legal relevance of lawmaking facts (descriptive grounds and axiological perspective). In this case, the inexorability of the truth of a proposition about the legal relevance of situations of state coercion is of the relatively *highest* degree.

## 3.3 An Example

If there is something whose importance Figure 1 was meant to flag, it is the claim that the intelligibility of disagreement about the degree of inexorability of truths about the legal relevance of state coercion is a direct function of the *absence* of background disagreement on how lawmaking facts become legally relevant. To illustrate how this correlation affects disagreement about the jurisprudential importance of state coercion, I conclude this Element with a contrastive examination of two pairs of competing claims derived from three comprehensive theories of law.[96]

To enable the contrastive examination of these theories we need to allocate to their respective quadrants each of the two tenets that make a theory eligible for representation by this model. The first tenet is a theory's position on the question of how lawmaking facts typically display their legal relevance. The second tenet is a theory's position on what makes situations of state coercion legally relevant.

---

[96] By 'comprehensive' I mean a theory that has a complete account of how lawmaking facts become legally relevant as well as how state coercion becomes legally relevant.

The taxonomisation of the first tenet will yield the theory's conception of a typically legal actuality, namely, the situation relative to which the degree of inexorability of the truth of claims about state coercion will be assessed. Legal actuality will be treated as a putatively correct description of the reality of how law is made.

The taxonomisation of the second tenet will yield the theory's conception of the maximal acceptable degree of departure of a situation of state coercion from the actuality of how law is made where a proposition about the legal relevance of situations of state coercion remains true. Depending on which theory is tested, such situation will differ from this actuality to varying degrees. The degree of inexorability of a proposition, $P$, about the legal relevance of situations of state coercion will be determined by how great a departure, in terms of similarity to the actuality of legally relevant lawmaking facts, is required for P to be falsified *not to be true*. The greater departure from the quadrant of lawmaking actuality is required for P to be falsified, the more secure or inexorable P's truth will turn out to be. With these background assumptions in place, I would like to preface the contrastive examination of the three example theories with a brief presentation of how each theory gets to be assigned to a particular quadrant on the coordinate plane.

### 3.3.1 Kantian Normative Positivism

As expected, the hardest taxonomic challenge is regarding the classification of Immanuel Kant's legal philosophy according to the contemporary jurisprudential inventory of taxonomic labels and relations. Reasons of dwindling space do not allow an exegetical digression into Kant's *Doctrine of Right*; hence, I will rely heavily on Arthur Ripstein's contemporary rendition of Kant's legal philosophy and confine my contribution to an overall characterisation of Kant's conception of law as an early variant of what is nowadays described as normative or ethical positivism.[97]

The basic marker that lends plausibility to this characterisation is the reversal Kant undertakes in the *Doctrine of Right* with regard to the relationship between morality and law. Instead of treating morality as a filter for weeding out the morally problematic or offensive aspects of actual institutional arrangements, Kant takes positive law to be a necessary and sufficient solution to immanent disagreement about what is just in the absence of a civil state (*Rechtsstaat*).[98]

---

[97] For a detailed defence of this interpretation, see Jeremy Waldron, *Kant's Legal Positivism*, 109 HARV. L. REV. 1535 (1996).

[98] Arthur Ripstein articulates Kant's idea of normative positive law noting that it 'makes private rights effective in space and time, by creating a standpoint through which omnilateral public law replaces unilateral private choice'. RIPSTEIN, *supra* note 35, at 306. *See also* Arthur Ripstein, *Kantian Legal Philosophy*, *in* A COMPANION TO PHILOSOPHY OF LAW AND LEGAL THEORY 392 (2d ed., Dennis Patterson ed., 2010).

Without positive law (*Lex*) a fundamental part of morality, namely, the attainment of equal external freedom under a universal law (*Ius*), is normatively impossible.

n light of this inevitably compressed exegesis, the Kantian variant of normative positivism can be interpreted as shouldering the following two commitments. First, both lawmaking power and coercive acts are individuated on *descriptive* grounds. Acts for making positive laws – what Kant calls 'external legislation' – are individuated as direct emanations of a legislative authority tasked with making the abstract duties of right determinate. Acts of state coercion are individuated as 'hinderings' of hindrances to external freedom, namely, to one's independence from the choices of others.[99] The grounds of their individuation are descriptive because their coercive character is not a function of their *pro tanto* wrongful effect but a function of their capacity to actually interfere with one's ability to set and pursue one's ends.[100] Such interference can be wrongful, as is the case with private wrongdoing, or it can be legitimate when the law sees to it that official interference with a prior wrongful interference restores a regime of equal freedom.

Second, the perspective from which Kant would assess the truth of propositions about the legal relevance of exercises of lawmaking power as determinations of abstract duties of right is the *axiological* perspective of an omnilateral will (*allseitige Willkür*). Public reason as omnilateral will provides a 'form of choice' by positing procedures through which laws can be made, applied and enforced. The perspective of public reason or the omnilateral will is axiological in the sense that it is motivated by the value of a negative state of affairs: the absence of unilateral violence which is the main mode of interaction in the state

---

[99] Kant describes the process by which such legally authorised 'hinderings' of hindrances to freedom are individuated by resorting to the spatial analogy of the mechanical interaction between opposing forces. Arthur Ripstein interprets his argument as suggesting that in much the same way that equivalent forces can cancel each other out,

the authorization to use coercion to hinder a hindrance to freedom is the use of force to 'destroy the consequence' of the initial hindrance, that is, to make it as though it had never happened ... any cancellation of the effects in space and time of any violation of this first set of reciprocal limits on freedom is itself *nothing more than the upholding of those very limits* [emphasis added]. Arthur Ripstein, *Hindering a Hindrance to Freedom*, 16 Jahrbuch Für Recht Und Ethik 227, 233 (2008).

[100] Arthur Ripstein contrasts the Kantian rationale of official coercion with the Benthamite tradition that individuates all instances of coercion as at least *pro tanto* wrongful; *see* Ripstein, *supra* note 35, at 55. Partly because he treats as marginal the importance of Kant's remarks about the descriptive individuation of independence-interfering acts in terms of spatial, external incompatibilities between the actions of embodied persons, Scott Anderson suggests that Ripstein's reading of Kant view is much closer to William Edmundson's deflationary account of legitimate legal enforcement as inherently non-coercive; *see* Anderson, *supra* note 92, at 29.

of nature. This normative defect can be repaired by establishing legal and political institutions that express an 'omnilateral will' in a set of legal directives.

By sharp contrast, the perspective from which Kant would assess the truth of propositions about the legal relevance of situations of state coercion is the *deontic* perspective of the special juridical relationships holding between private persons (property, contract and status rights). What fuses these relationships into a global normative perspective is their potential to become sources of duties and rights that uphold the value of equal freedom. It is from within the perspective of treating such relationships as sources of duties and rights that Kant determines the legal relevance of publicly authorised coercion. Situations of coercion are legally relevant when and because there obtains a legally enforceable and unconditional duty to enter and remain in a civil or rightful condition that will make juridical relationships of property, contract and status permissibly enforceable.[101]

### 3.3.2 Dworkinian Interpretivism

Ronald Dworkin's legal interpretivist theory holds that lawmaking practices and acts of state coercion are *jointly* individuated on the same *normative* grounds. Political decisions aimed at making law ('legislation'), as well judicial and administrative practices that apply and enforce past political decisions, are treated as alternating manifestations of the responsibility of government to impose limits on the coercive distributive effects of its policies on the benefits and burdens of life in a political society. These coercive distributive effects can be broadly construed as any type of collectively upheld interference 'with citizens' options so as to leave them no decent option but take the action the interference was meant to lead them to take'.[102] Pending *further* normative argument, such interference is normatively individuated as *pro tanto* wrongful, *thereby* necessitating a special justification of its principled consistency with past institutional practice.

On this scheme, both political decisions and coercive state practices are constitutive elements of law. Departing somewhat from Dworkin's jurisprudential

---

[101] For the relationship between the legal relevance of state coercion and the perspective of a pre-civil condition, see Section 1.2.

[102] Stavropoulos, *supra* note 36, at 352. For a legal interpretivist, any governmental action that conveys a claim to eliminate some alternatives or make them non-viable is a form of action-direction that, without additional justification of its relation to past institutional practice, is *pro tanto* wrongful, *hence* coercive. In corroboration of the interpretivist individuation of coercion in terms of the justifiability of its *pro tanto* wrongness, Stavropoulos cites Nozick's argument from coercion noting that '[in] order to assess whether some action is coercive and objectionable or at least deserving moral scrutiny, we need to step back and consider the transition from the subject's situation before the interference to the results of the interference'. *Id.* at 341.

idiolect we could say that Dworkinian lawmaking facts are to be understood as facts about the culmination of certain institutional practices in decisions that affect or purport to affect the content of enforceable claims of right or duty. Dworkinian facts about state coercion are facts about the effective power of institutions to use force or otherwise coercively direct citizens' action. *Both* types of fact are legally relevant in the same sense that they enable or trigger the instantiation of abstract principles of egalitarian distributive and procedural justice by more particular obligations and rights. This triggering occurs in a circular fashion when the more particular obligations and rights flowing from triggered principles turn out to be consistent with *both* lawmaking and state coercion–related facts in a way that best justifies the entire institutional record of a political community.[103]

Moreover, the normative perspective that justifies judgements about such proper triggering is the *deontic* perspective of a 'protestant interpreter' of the law. This is the perspective of an agent who treats the non-voluntary, associative relationship between citizens and their government as a source of special obligations and responsibilities. Each and every member of a political community is invited to adopt this critical perspective towards the responsibilities of government vis-à-vis its citizens. This perspective is taken to be essential to a people 'united in community but divided in project, interest, and conviction' and conveys a moral demand of governmental officials to treat all members of a political community with equal concern and respect.[104] As Nicos Stavropoulos remarks, this is the perspective that 'falls out of a theory of *special obligations of role*, which in turn is part of a more general theory of moral responsibility' [emphasis added].[105] The responsibilities that citizens and government officials acquire in the relevant associative context are supposed to be such that they are in line with the scheme of principle that justifies the institutional record of their community.

### 3.3.3 Razian Exclusive Positivism

Joseph Raz's theory of law is articulated in the language of political authority, construed as the state's normative power to impose duties on its subjects. The

---

[103] *See* DWORKIN, *supra* note 36, at 225–75.

[104] DWORKIN, *supra* note 36, at 413. Gerald Postema believes that Dworkin's Protestantism goes far beyond this reflective viewpoint that every citizen should be urged to take in interpreting what the content of the law requires in particular circumstances. For a critical account of Dworkin's interpretive 'protestantism', see Gerald Postema, *"Protestant" Interpretation and Social Practices*, 6 LAW AND PHILOSOPHY 283 (1987).

[105] Nicos Stavropoulos, *Why Principles?*, Oxford Legal Studies Research Paper No. 28/2007 (Oct. 2007), 21, https://ssrn.com/abstract=1023758.

perspective from which exercises of such authority become legally relevant both in terms of lawmaking and coercive enforcement is the *axiological* perspective of perfectionist liberalism.[106] According to this viewpoint, political institutions are supposed to improve the lives of citizens by serving their needs and helping them to live better, more valuable lives than they would be able to do in their absence.

Political authority is normally justified, Raz suggests, when 'the alleged subject is likely better to comply with reasons which apply to him ... if he accepts the directives of the alleged authority as authoritatively binding and tries to follow them, rather than by trying to follow the reasons which apply to him directly'.[107] Whereas this type of authority is practical or duty-imposing, its grounds are distinctly theoretical or probabilistic. Such practical–political authority is legitimate only if its subjects are *more likely* to act as practical reason requires by following the authority's directives.[108] Consequently, the legally distinctive way in which modern states tap into the grounds or source of that authority is, as Raz argues, by *claiming* it, that is, by representing it as legitimately possessed.[109] '[T]hough a legal system may not have legitimate authority, or though its legitimate authority may not be as extensive as it claims', Raz notes, 'every legal system *claims* that it possesses legitimate authority' [emphasis added].[110] It is because legal systems, through their officials, respond to the source of their authority by way of publicly claiming its legitimate possession that the axiological perspective of Razian authority encodes a specific conception of public reason as the authoritative facilitation of goodness-tracking exercises of individual autonomy.[111]

---

[106] Raz describes his view as perfectionist. *See* Joseph Raz, *Autonomy, Toleration, and the Harm Principle, in* ISSUES IN CONTEMPORARY LEGAL PHILOSOPHY 313, 331–32 (Ruth Gavison ed., 1987).

[107] RAZ, *supra* note 21, at 53.

[108] Raz clarifies that the normal justification only grounds a legitimate claim of authority provided it does not undermine the alleged subject's personal autonomy. In his words, 'if both the normal justification thesis and the condition of autonomy are fulfilled then, in general, the alleged authority is legitimate'. Joseph Raz, *Facing Up*, 62 *S.* CAL. L. REV. 1153, 1181 (1988).

[109] Raz notes that the more particular ways in which legal officials claim possession of legitimate political authority are evidenced

> by the fact that legal institutions are officially designated as 'authorities,' by the fact that they regard themselves as having the right to impose obligations on their subjects, by their claims that their subjects owe them allegiance, and that their subjects ought to obey the law as it requires to be obeyed (i.e. in all cases except those in which some legal doctrine justifies breach of duty). Raz, *supra* note 60, at 215–16.

[110] *Id.* at 215.

[111] That is, ways of exercising one's personal autonomy that track the good (rather than right)-making characteristics of actions.

Both exercises of lawmaking power and of the power of coercive enforcement are descriptively individuated as different modes of authoritative action-direction.[112] More specifically, certain utterances are individuated as legally valid directives on descriptive, source-based considerations. A basic prerequisite that any legislative utterance must satisfy in order to be legally valid is that it must be possible to identify its existence and content without relying on the normative considerations on which it purports to adjudicate.[113] Such identification or individuation takes place on exclusively – ergo the label exclusive positivism – descriptive grounds.

Acts of authoritative enforcement, on the other hand, are also individuated as legally coercive on descriptive, probabilistic grounds. Their coerciveness is determined by reference to a non-ideal baseline set by the comparative claim that the law subject's post-coercion situation would be worse than the non-ideal baseline of what *would be more likely* to have happened if she had decided to act conformably with a legal directive. The subject's *ex ante* situation – namely, prior to coercive enforcement – would be such that it would be *more likely* for the law subject to act for the right kind of reasons if she had decided to treat the legal directive as settling the question of what to do. The subject's *ex post* situation, where certain sanctions have been officially imposed, is such that it *is more unlikely* that someone acted for the right kind of reasons despite the authoritative, direct or remedial, enforcement of the violated directive.[114] In other words, the epistemic foundation of Raz's conception of legal authority is such that state coercion is individuated as a mode of coercive direction of action whose occurrence significantly *increases the probability* that the law subject has failed to act conformably with what practical reason requires, independently of

---

[112] The legislative mode of authoritative action-direction consists in *telling* people what to do, whereas the coercive mode consists in *getting* people to do what they were told to do.

[113] Raz, *supra* note 60, at 218.

[114] Only if the directive has patently failed to correctly weigh on the reasons that apply to a certain question will it be the case that, despite the infliction of a legal sanction, it remains more likely that the law subject was, nonetheless, right in having acted for one of the first-order reasons that counted *against* the prescribed act. There has been a gradual shift in Raz's view about the type of first-order reasons that are subject to exclusion. In the second edition of *Practical Reason and Norms*, Raz suggests that 'one ought to exclude all the reasons both for and against [the prescribed act] which were within the jurisdiction of the authority'. Raz, *supra* note 17, at 191. In later work he confines the scope of exclusion to first-order reasons against an act prescribed by a rule claiming that '[t]he service conception [of authority] expresses that thought by the thesis that authoritative directives preempt those reasons against the conduct they require that the authority was meant to take into account in deciding to issue its directives'. Joseph Raz, *The Problem of Authority: Revisiting the Service Conception*, 90 MINN. L. REV. 1003, 1018 (2006). For a critical account of Raz's oscillation regarding the scope of exclusion, see Christopher Essert, *A Dilemma for Protected Reasons*, 31 LAW AND PHILOSOPHY 49 (2012).

the violated directive and independently of its coercive enforcement. Such failure registers the attribution of a certain kind of irrationality to scofflaws.

The normative perspective through which legal officials coercively (judicially and administratively) interact with the members of a political community is the axiological perspective of perfectionist liberalism. Acts of judicial or executive enforcement also become legally relevant as ways of getting people to do what legal edicts antecedently require them to do. Both lawmaking and state coercion are represented as ways of leading law subjects to comply with what practical reason antecedently requires of them.

### 3.3.4 Contrasting Raz with Kant

Let us begin with the *Raz–Kant* pair. Whereas Raz licenses the inclusion of both lawmaking and state coercion in the same *descriptive–axiological* quadrant, Kant approaches state coercion in a way that departs from the actuality of lawmaking. The reason is that for Kant as well as for Kantian legal philosophers, coercion acquires its pre-eminent relevance in the *pre-civil* scenario where a civil or rightful condition has not yet been established and private agents attempt to address each other and unilaterally impose claims of lawful possession of different things. In a 'state of nature' and without the legitimation of public institutions, all rights are provisionally had; hence they are not permissibly enforceable. Only unilateral violence is possible.[115] It is from within the pre-civil perspective of legally underenforced special relationships (property, contract, status) that the provisional status of the rights and duties based on such relationships becomes legally relevant. It becomes relevant in the sense that it grounds a legal duty to render the possession of such rights definitive and secure.

This assurance requires of denizens of a natural state to transition into a rightful condition that will include executive institutions tasked with the provision of compelling assurance that no one will be treated as a mere means by others because others will eventually be led to comply with their duties of

---

[115] Arthur Ripstein elucidates Kant's counterfactual argument noting that

> rights to external objects in a state of nature are merely *provisional*, because they are all titles to coerce that *nobody is entitled to enforce coercively*. A provisional property right is thus a right to use force to exclude others from an external object while you are in possession of it; although physical possession gives provisional title, in anticipation of a condition in which rights can be made conclusive, your entitlement to use force is limited to the case in which interfering with your possession thereby interferes with your person. Any other use of force to secure an object against another is just aggression against that person, which can be resisted with right [emphasis added]. RIPSTEIN, *supra* note 35, at 165.

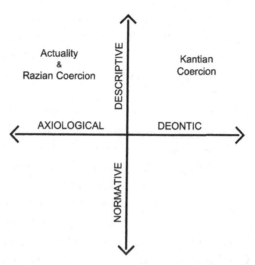

**Figure 2** Commensurating 'Razian' and 'Kantian' coercion

right. The joint application of these considerations results in choosing the *descriptive–deontic* quadrant as the fitting habitat for Kant's account of state coercion. The combined allocation of the lawmaking and state coercion claims advanced by Raz and Kant yields a taxonomic result that makes disagreement between them over the jurisprudential importance of state coercion meaningful. Figure 2 makes this result accessible pictorially.

Raz and Kant apply the same standards for determining the legally typical actuality of how lawmaking facts become legally relevant. This is depicted by the common assignment of this actuality in the *descriptive–axiological*, upper-left quadrant. According to both theories, authoritative directives and positive laws, respectively, are direct emanations of exercises of political authority; the legal relevance of such exercises is settled by applying the axiological perspective of those officials who represent their lawmaking power as valuable in a certain way (Raz's normal justification thesis and Kant's omnilateral will, respectively). Nevertheless, this pair of theories remains substantially divided on the question regarding the degree of inexorability of the truth of the proposition that state coercion is legally relevant.

Raz treats state coercion as a dispensable aspect of law, as evidenced by the assignment of its relevant position in the *same* quadrant as the one where the actuality of lawmaking resides. In other words, Raz does not license a coercive situation whose configuration even minimally departs from the way in which lawmaking facts about the exercise of legal authority actually become legally relevant to be a situation where state coercion *preserves* its jurisprudential importance. In Raz's famous hypothetical scenario, the addressees of authoritative directives are not humans but angelic beings whose religious virtue inclines them to unexceptionally obey the law. Within such a quasi-religious political community authoritative guidance would still be required but only on a voluntary, non-coercive basis.

While the situation where state coercion *remains* legally relevant is configured by the same criteria as those that apply to the actuality of lawmaking, the angelic scenario which deprives state coercion of its legal relevance would fall within the *descriptive–deontic* – rather than the descriptive–axiological – quadrant. In a society where law is made for angels, instead of humans, the perspective that would make authoritative legal guidance relevant would not be the axiological perspective of perfectionist liberalism but the *deontic* perspective of the special obligations arising within a quasi-religious community. Angels would be legally obligated to follow the directives of their officials in virtue of their role as insiders to a practice that fastidiously excludes scofflaws from its jurisdiction. Moreover, in the same angelic scenario, authoritative directives would still be individuated on the same descriptive grounds as in the actuality of lawmaking.

These remarks are meant to show that the proposed taxonomic model is generic enough to be used for the different task of identifying the degree of inexorability of the truth of propositions about the legal relevance of *lawmaking*. The conceivability of this scenario where state coercion loses its legal relevance *but* lawmaking preserves its legal relevance is also an indication that, by the lights of Raz's theory of law, the truth of the proposition that authoritative directives addressed to angelic citizens remain legally relevant by providing reasons to treat them as settling the question of what to do is inexorable to a *moderate* degree, precisely because the ontological grounds for individuating exercises of legal authority remain the same (descriptive). In other words, whereas, according to Raz, we cannot imagine the angelic scenario as a situation where state coercion remains legally relevant, we *can* imagine the same scenario as a situation where lawmaking facts preserve their legal relevance, albeit in a modified sense. For Raz, the angelic scenario is a *legal* scenario – we still have a 'case of law' – with no legally relevant state coercion.

By contrast, the Kantian claim about the legal relevance of state coercion has a moderate degree of inexorability as evidenced by the fact that it resides in a quadrant (*descriptive–deontic*) that differs from the actuality of lawmaking only with respect to the applicable normative–practical perspective (equal freedom between private agents). The Kantian situation of state coercion retains its weightier ontological similarity to the actuality of lawmaking as both acts of state coercion and lawmaking acts are individuated on descriptive grounds. The only difference from lawmaking actuality is that in the counterfactual scenario of a pre-civil state there is no deontic perspective that can ascribe finality to social attempts to impose and, subsequently, enforce regulations on the special relationships that are formed within a 'state of nature'.

The resulting picture is that the dispute between a Razian exclusive positivist and a Kantian normative positivist is an instance of substantive political disagreement that takes place within the broader territory of *political liberalism* under two of its major competing guises, perfectionism (Raz) and contractualism (Kant). This is a robust and substantial disagreement. Its object concerns the *normativity* – not the ontology – of state coercion and, more precisely, the principles that should govern its use. For a Kantian, such liberal principles are of a distinctly contractualist nature, whereas for a Razian positivist the applicable liberal principles are grounded in perfectionist considerations. The Kantian legitimation of state coercion comes through agreement on the necessity of reciprocal limits on individual freedom. The Razian legitimation of state coercion emanates from the instrumental value of authoritative guidance as a means of ensuring that members of a political community will lead better, more flourishing lives.

### 3.3.5 Contrasting Dworkin with Kant

An opposite verdict is reached if we attempt to adjudicate a hypothetical jurisprudential dispute between Kant and Dworkin. In this case the disagreement about the jurisprudential importance of state coercion is verbal or merely apparent for a reason that can be easily inferred from Figure 3.

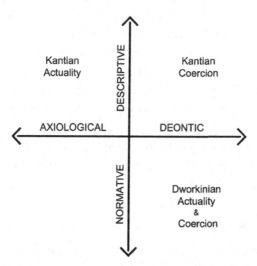

**Figure 3** Commensurating 'Kantian' and 'Dworkinian' coercion

Dworkin and Kant do not use a common framework for theorising about the typically legal actuality of how law is made. Without prior adjudication of this more fundamental dispute, it makes no sense to try to adjudge which theory attributes the proper degree of inexorability to the truth of a proposition about the legal relevance of state coercion. It makes no sense because metric disagreements are disagreements about how far certain situations are allowed to depart or differ from one, common point of origin without ceasing to obtain. In our case, this point of origin is legal actuality construed as the actuality of how law is made. No common origin, thus no measurement to disagree about.

Kant understands legislation as an institutional determination of the abstract principles of right (*Rechtsprinzipien*) on which an abstract system of equal freedom is founded. A legal interpretivist portrays legislation as part of a broader institutional practice that, when it merits claims of right or duty, triggers – rather than makes more determinate – principles of egalitarian distributive justice. For the former, the content of the law is the content of positive laws, or equivalently, of posited rules, whereas for the latter the content of the law is the content of generalisable claims of duty or right that are fitting responses to certain aspects of past institutional practice.[116]

The upshot of this fundamental difference between the two example theories is that they define the actuality of lawmaking in sharply distinct ways. The Kantian actuality of lawmaking is composed of posited – hence, descriptively identifiable – laws which are legally relevant by virtue of their operating as authoritative determinations of the domains of action of which each individual remains in charge in a way that upholds equal freedom. This relevance is ascribed from within the axiological perspective of an omnilateral will whose exercise is meant to repair the defect of unilateral violence.[117]

Conversely, the interpretivist actuality of lawmaking is composed of facts about the grounding of claims of legal right or obligation in past institutional decisions and standing practices of government which are legally relevant when and because they trigger principles of egalitarian justice that, in their turn, justify institutional practice. The perspective that ascribes this legal relevance to principles is the deontic perspective of the 'protestant interpreter' who treats her relationship to government as grounding the demand to treat people with equal concern and respect.[118]

---

[116] Crucially, these claims become generalisable when and because they properly fit past institutional practice.

[117] This is not the Razian action-guiding authority of telling people what to do, but the constitutive authority of delimitating personal practical authority.

[118] DWORKIN, *supra* note 36, at 134.

Whereas Kantian normative positivism assigns moderate inexorability to state coercion, legal interpretivism is depicted as *denying* that state coercion – surprise, surprise – is an indispensable feature of law! It appears that, according to the latter theory, there is no scenario that is even minimally different from the way legal actuality is constituted where state coercion *retains* its jurisprudential importance. This is not an oddity that the model mistakenly represents as an expected outcome, or so I would like to argue. One formally acceptable way to read this result is to assert that, according to legal interpretivism, state coercion is a *contingent* aspect of law. But this reading totally misses the interpretivist rationale that makes state coercion counterfactually undetachable – hence, contingent – from the actuality of how institutional practice becomes legally relevant.

From the viewpoint of a legal interpretivist any depiction of law that departs from the actuality portrayed by what Dworkin calls the 'doctrinal concept' of law is a *sociologically* but not jurisprudentially informative modal statement. The doctrinal concept of law is the concept we use when we ask what the law is in a given jurisdiction. The pervasiveness of state coercion in actual political communities, according to Dworkin, assigns priority to the justification of coercive institutional practices. That being said, this priority must not be understood as a modal claim of necessity but as a normative claim of explanatory relevance.[119] Consequently, any scenario where institutional practice – which Dworkin treats as a union of political decisions, doctrinal argument and coercive enforcement – is not an occasion for a principled limitation of recourse to state coercion, is a scenario whose articulation is informed by what Dworkin calls the 'sociological concept' of law.[120] The implication of this distinction between the doctrinal and sociological concepts of law is that the claim that state coercion is only contingently legally relevant is a true *sociological*, but not jurisprudential claim.

The sociological flavour of the claim that the proposed model supports is the result of Dworkin's metanormative objection to the meaningfulness of jurisprudential claims cast in modal or, more generally, metaphysical language. His view is that modal statements about law's necessary features or metric statements about law's degree of coerciveness are always made from within a sociological viewpoint; hence they are not statements whose truth can be

---

[119] For the application of the doctrinal concept of law, see Ronald Dworkin, Justice in Robes 13–18 (2006).

[120] Dworkin offers a description rather than a definition of different concepts of law. Regarding the sociological concept of law he remarks that 'we use "law" to name a particular type of institutional social structure. We might ask, for instance, using that sociological concept, when law first appeared in primitive tribal societies, or whether commerce is possible without law.' *Id.* at 3.

evaluated on jurisprudential or, equivalently, legal philosophical grounds.[121] Because nothing of philosophical importance, Dworkin argues, turns on whether we classify a counterfactually modified system as a legal system, it makes no *jurisprudential* sense to ponder whether state coercion or any other feature of governance by law is necessary or contingent. What matters is the best total justification of actual legal practice.

---

[121] In Dworkin's words,

> [h]ow universal can an interpretive theory of legal doctrine be? Suppose we set out to construct an interpretation of legal practice that would fit everything we took to fall under our sociological concept of law. How much detail could that highly abstract interpretation contain? Perhaps very little: it may be that once we begin the process any interpretive steps we take automatically make our interpretive account more parochial ... So I suppose the best answer to the question of whether my theory of law is meant to be universal or parochial is: both. *Id.* at 231.

## Cambridge Elements ≡

# Philosophy of Law

## Series Editors

### George Pavlakos
*University of Glasgow*

George Pavlakos is Professor of Law and Philosophy at the School of Law, University of Glasgow. He has held visiting posts at the universities of Kiel and Luzern, the European University Institute, the UCLA Law School, the Cornell Law School and the Beihang Law School in Beijing. He is the author of *Our Knowledge of the Law* (2007) and more recently has co-edited *Agency, Negligence and Responsibility* (2021) and *Reasons and Intentions in Law and Practical Agency* (2015).

### Gerald J. Postema
*University of North Carolina at Chapel Hill*

Gerald J. Postema is Professor Emeritus of Philosophy at the University of North Carolina at Chapel Hill. Among his publications count *Utility, Publicity, and Law: Bentham's Moral and Legal Philosophy* (2019); *On the Law of Nature, Reason, and the Common Law: Selected Jurisprudential Writings of Sir Matthew Hale* (2017); *Legal Philosophy in the Twentieth Century: The Common Law World* (2011), *Bentham and the Common Law Tradition*, 2nd edition (2019).

### Kenneth M. Ehrenberg
*University of Surrey*

Kenneth M. Ehrenberg is Reader in Public Law and Legal Theory at the University of Surrey School of Law and Co-Director of the Surrey Centre for Law and Philosophy. He is the author of *The Functions of Law* (2016) and numerous articles on the nature of law, jurisprudential methodology, the relation of law to morality, practical authority, and the epistemology of evidence law.

## Associate Editor

Sally Zhu
*University of Sheffield*

Sally Zhu is a Lecturer in Property Law at University of Sheffield. Her research is on property and private law aspects of platform and digital economies.

## About the Series

This series provides an accessible overview of the philosophy of law, drawing on its varied intellectual traditions in order to showcase the interdisciplinary dimensions of jurisprudential enquiry, review the state of the art in the field, and suggest fresh research agendas for the future. Focussing on issues rather than traditions or authors, each contribution seeks to deepen our understanding of the foundations of the law, ultimately with a view to offering practical insights into some of the major challenges of our age.

Cambridge Elements ≡

# Philosophy of Law

## Elements in the Series

Printed in the United States
by Baker & Taylor Publisher Services